To the memory of

Frank and Olive Hare,

and

Paul Portelli.

TABLE OF CONTENTS

Preface

The guiding idea behind this collection of essays is to offer a stimulating and up-to-date introduction to a wide range of educational, pedagogical, and curricular aims, principles, ideals and approaches which are keenly debated at the present time. The editors mapped out a list of central questions, focusing on those topics likely to be of most concern to anyone interested in education and schooling today, especially teachers, student teachers, and administrators, but also members of the general public. Leading commentators were invited to contribute a short, original essay that would draw readers into the current discussion in the field. Each author worked independently, but inevitably many important connections and related themes emerge among the papers, illustrating the fact that these topics constitute a network of ideas such that an understanding gained in one area casts light on issues raised elsewhere. The result is that these essays can serve not only as an excellent introduction to each individual topic but can also collectively provide a general overview of a wide area of contemporary educational theory.

Many familiar educational ideas have a puzzling and elusive aspect that is common to all philosophical concepts. They represent certain fundamental human qualities and attainments that readily lend themselves to rival interpretations and emphases. Dewey reminds us that they are commonly emblazoned on the banner of particular educational movements and ideologies. Imagination, critical thinking, knowledge, scientific understanding, wisdom, and open-mindedness are often put forward as educational ideals and their very familiarity and intuitive appeal makes it difficult to look at them afresh; we come to them with many assumptions and associations already in place. How are these general aims to be understood? How do they relate to the notion of education itself? Why are they thought to be important? How do we evaluate conflicting accounts about their nature and value? How are we to deal with skeptical views, such as those associated with postmodernism, about the possibility and desirability of these general aims? Is it important for teachers to think carefully about these ideals?

We might wonder if a philosophical account of such ideals can give us any guidance with respect to how they might be pursued and exemplified.

Inquiry in the classroom, discussion methods, the exploration of controversial issues, and constructivist approaches are popularly advanced as pedagogically desirable, but what do these ideas amount to? How do these approaches relate to the general idea of teaching itself? To what extent are educational ideals embedded in these strategies? When they are attempted in practice, how far does the classroom reality reflect the philosophical ideal? Is it possible to set out guidelines and criteria that would help teachers recognize when genuine inquiry and discussion are occurring in their classrooms and suggest ways in which their practice might approximate these norms more closely?

Inspired by these reflections, we might begin to formulate an ideal of good teaching. Is a good teacher someone committed to progressive education? What is involved in that notion? Can the idea of authority be reconciled with good teaching? Do the notions of critical and feminist pedagogy help us to understand the nature of good teaching? To what extent should teachers embrace the ideal of freedom of speech? How do the principles embedded in professionalism and leadership help us to articulate an account of good teaching? Is it necessary for us to rethink our approaches to teacher education in the light of these ideas?

Certain ideas emerge from time to time that seem to many to capture something vitally important to the whole educational enterprise, reaching beyond particular subjects in the curriculum and beyond particular methods of teaching. These would include: education for social justice, multiculturalism, anti-racism, and citizenship; education for democratic values, avoidance of indoctrination, and media literacy; an emphasis on caring and student engagement, and an education that nurtures character and spirituality. These are complex ideas but often invoked as if their meaning and value could be taken for granted. Why have these ideals and aims emerged as central? What reasons can be offered to show their significance if that were to be doubted? Are all of these ideals mutually compatible? How do we prevent them from degenerating into mere watchwords and clichés? The essays on these topics attempt to illuminate the values that enrich these ideals, and to show how education and teaching might be transformed if they were taken seriously.

These overarching ideals seek, in part, to capture some insight into what makes a good school. Other questions spring to mind once the idea of good schooling comes into focus. To what extent should schooling aim at vocational education? What are the problems and issues relating to schooling in the contemporary, urban environment? At the same time, there are certain trends today that are thought by many to seriously detract from the ideal of a good school. Is the present emphasis on accountability in education desirable? What should we think about what is called the marketization of education? Should our schools introduce zero tolerance policies? If we are inclined to react negatively to these ideas, can we articulate what our concern is? What is the motivation behind the movements which endorse these practices? Russell reminds us that if an idea seems to us obviously absurd, we need to find out how it ever came to *seem* true to intelligent people. What reasons are offered in support of these ideas?

At the very outset of Western philosophy, Aristotle produced a philosophical lexicon of thirty complex and disputed terms; this collection of essays contributes to the same philosophical tradition of examination and clarification of problematic ideas. Each of these essays is introduced by a question to underline the fact that the topic remains the subject of considerable debate. A brief section of further readings at the end of each essay indicates where the discussion can be followed up. It is often remarked that all of these notions are contested, meaning that no definitive account that avoids controversy can be given. Our hope is that this collection will help readers to determine how far agreement can be reached, to understand the nature and the source of disagreement where it exists, and to formulate their own views on these questions.

Our thanks to all of the contributors for sharing our belief in this project, to Trevor Norris for editorial assistance, to Niki Hare for proofreading, and to Antony Hare for the cover design. In every respect, this work has been a joint effort of both editors.

William Hare
John P. Portelli

July 2005

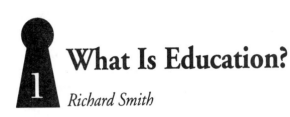

What Is Education?

Richard Smith

The first point to make is that this apparently innocent question does not permit a straightforward reply. It cannot be answered with a dictionary definition, for instance, partly because any adequate dictionary lists many alternative and contradictory senses of the word, and partly because 'education' is a word people adopt to describe their own preferred ideas of what should take place in schools, universities and elsewhere. No-one is likely to set out their own vision of these things and acknowledge that it is not educational. In this respect, 'education' is like 'democracy' or 'culture' in being what some have called "an essentially contested concept".

Education has been identified as the inculcation of basic skills at one extreme and in terms of more high-flown ideals concerned with civilized thinking and behaviour at the other. There is, however, a case for saying that there is something distinctive and unique about education worth the name, and therefore that education cannot be unproblematically identified with whatever goes on in the institutions set up to provide it, since it is always possible to complain that a school, for example, is not properly educating its pupils, though it may be instructing them and improving their knowledge and skills. It would seem odd to say that children were being educated if they were being taught to bully, or if they were learning how to make instruments of torture.

Education certainly has the function of meeting the needs of the society of which it is a part, whether these are expressed in economic terms as a matter of equipping the workforce with relevant skills and capacities or in broader terms of inducting young people into cultural and moral norms. Where, as in most countries in the twenty-first century, the state is the principal sponsor of education, its interest in ensuring that these needs are met is entirely legitimate. Education may also be said to aim at the development of knowledge and understanding, in a way that no other institution does; at helping individuals achieve their potential, live richer lives or find their paths to personal fulfilment; at fostering their capacity for rational and critical autonomy, for independence of mind and action. There is also a skeptical view that a principal function of education is to depress the expectations and ambitions of those many young people to whom our societies will not be able to offer rewarding and satisfying work.

It is immediately clear that many of the functions noted above are incompatible. If the state requires docile wage-slaves in factories and call-centres, then there cannot be unrestrained development of critical autonomy. Although we want children to be initiated into the moral and cultural norms of their society, we also want them to question and even to oppose these norms in cases where these include for instance racism, bullying or homophobia. It must also be noted that sometimes education is, or has been, conceived in ways that do not accord with what may seem to be simple commonsense. Not everybody is now likely to be comfortable with the idea that education should instill manliness or patriotism, or that it is an essentially spiritual process, for example.

There has nevertheless been a fair measure of consensus in the western tradition of educational thinking that 'education' indicates a process through which learners expand their intellectual horizons and become initiated into the various kinds of knowledge and understanding that are worthwhile or, as it is sometimes put, learn to speak the languages (such as those of science, mathematics, and the arts) that make up the conversation of humankind. The German word *Bildung* connotes just such an enterprise of encouraging pupils and students to rise above their local and particular circumstances, and to achieve the self-directedness and the understanding of universal moral and aesthetic principles that constitute the attainment of authentic humanity. This is an essentially *liberal* vision of education as a process that frees the learner from the contingencies of the world that he or she happens to have been born into, opening up a realm of wider ideas and values. In this sense education is often said to be an end in itself, by contrast with training which consists in the acquisition of skills that are means towards ends – ends such as gaining qualifications, driving a car or earning a living. Sometimes this is expressed by saying that the value of education is *intrinsic*. Education properly so called is thus guided by norms and ideals internal to the very idea of education and not laid down from outside by individuals, governments or other bodies.

In the modern world, the language of instrumental or technical reason predominates. It foregrounds rational planning and values such as efficiency and effectiveness; it talks of the 'bottom line' and of maximizing the input-output ratio. This language, familiar from government and official publications, naturally leads to thinking about the nature of education in a particular way. It suggests that the sensible question to ask about education is just what its aims are, so that the appropriate answer will come in the form of a list, probably set out in bullet-points. Some things however cannot be treated in this language without doing violence to them: not only education, but friendship, the arts and the natural world, for example. They show us that means-end reasoning alone will not do, for our dawning or changing sense of the value of education or the natural world stands precisely to challenge our instrumentally conceived and generally short-term aims in life.

The question just what education is, then, is to be treated with caution. The ideal of education as having intrinsic value cannot be conclusively demonstrated. We can only depict it as best we can and ask others to test it against their own intuitions about the highest things that human beings are capable of and how they might be prepared to achieve them. Handled in this way, the very process of thinking about education is itself properly educative.

Further Readings

Marples, R., (Ed.) (1999) *The Aims of Education*. London: Routledge.

Maskell, D., (1999) Education, Education, Education: or, What Has Jane Austen to Teach Tony Blunkett?, *Journal of Philosophy of Education* 33 (2): 157-74.

Oakeshott, M., (1972) Education: The Engagement and its Frustration, in R. F. Dearden, P. H. Hirst and R. S. Peters (Eds), *Education and the Development of Reason*. London: Routledge & Kegan Paul, 19-49.

What Is Wisdom?

Brenda Almond

Is it the business of education to promote wisdom, or simply to cultivate cleverness? Or does this depend on the age of the learner and the stage of education? And what indeed is the difference between being wise and being clever? It is easy to see why these questions are fundamental to an understanding of education, for wisdom is something people need for sound decision-making, not only in the public world of politics and business, but also in personal life. Wisdom involves accepting the stabilizing constraints of reason and rationality, but it is a richer concept than these, involving feeling as well as intellectual judgment. It is often said that wisdom is something that only life itself can bring. Even so, young children can often show an innate wisdom that their elders have lost in the battle for success, career advancement or self-promotion. A wise teacher will seek to preserve and foster that, or at least try not to crush it at that early growing stage.

There are wisdom traditions in the world's great cultures and religions. Ancient Egyptian teachings have been found from as early as 2,500 BC. Later, Chinese Confucianism, Buddhism, Hinduism and the Hebrew sages of the Old Testament all offered maxims and counsels for the conduct of life. Past philosophers in the Western tradition also had something to say about these matters; indeed, 'philosophy' is the ancient word for the love of wisdom and it was philosophers who set up the first 'academy' or university in Athens in the fifth century BC. Philosophy today, though, is often more concerned with slickness and skill in argument than with answering the question 'how to live.'

This can be partly explained by the fact that both philosophers and educators in the liberal democracies rightly take pride in the freedom they enjoy to approach subjects of study in an open and critical way and so try to avoid any appearance of dogmatism. But criticism is not a value in itself. If it is to generate wisdom, it has to be accompanied by humility and a recognition of your own limitations. Some parts of the world have different learning traditions in which classical authors and texts are studied for the insights they can offer rather than for any errors they may have made, and this contrasts with the Western tendency to criticize and attack the writers and thinkers central to its traditions. But in education, this may not do as much to encourage freedom of thought as it appears. For the critical approach often trades in what are no more than standard criticisms which must themselves be learnt, while genuine originality continues to earn *nul points*.

True wisdom comes from something deeper and more intuitive than any of this. It involves, too, a kind of empathy, not only with other people, but with the natural world in which we find ourselves. Wisdom can be linked to the perennial search for meaning in life, summed up in the question, "What is it all for?" As such, it is the quest for order, plan, purpose and method in the face of the arbitrary contingency of the world and of events. For the Stoic Roman emperor Marcus Aurelius, as later for Spinoza, the seventeenth century Dutch philosopher, this quest is best met by accepting the inevitability of things, not wasting time resenting or fearing the course of events, but recognizing that all that happens is bound into a web of causes and consequences. For the Stoics, this meant learning to live free from emotional attachments, but perhaps a braver conclusion from such a philosophical view, would be to engage with the world, while accepting the inevitable disappointments that will bring.

So wisdom need not be understood as an exclusively metaphysical concept. On the contrary, it is better understood as in some way connecting with the choices people make in their personal lives – choices such as those of lifestyle, partner, place, or career that form the stuff and substance of an individual life. For it is in close personal relationships – whether between adults or between parents and children – that many people find meaning for their lives. But wise private choices do in the end make for wise public and community life, while large-scale carelessness in the personal life of individuals can lead to the disintegration or unraveling of the social fabric.

This understanding of wisdom can have implications for the curriculum: in history studies, for example, it would mean looking to the past and being willing to learn from it. It would mean learning to transcend the narrow limitations of our own time – to look backwards and to think forwards.

Of course, many studies – science, mathematics, foreign languages - involve learning facts and acquiring skills and this may seem to place them at a greater distance from the reflective approach that characterizes wisdom, for this is sometimes defined as being concerned with ends rather than means. But science and technology are not *only* about means; they can open the door to an understanding of the world we live in, just as well-chosen literature can make up for the limited experience one person's life can provide, while a foreign language well-learnt can be an initiation into the history and culture of another society.

At whatever level, then, and in whatever area academic studies are taken, they form a background for the kind of humanistic, and even spiritual, wisdom that studies more directly focused on the human person can foster. But educators may find a more realistic goal in aiming to promote the day-to-day wisdom people need in their daily lives. This need not be too limited or narrow an approach if it is part of a broader ethical perspective that promotes moral sensitivity rather than moral nihilism or a shallow utilitarianism. For this in itself could provide the ground from which learners may choose to set out on the path to philosophical wisdom in its deeper sense – that which ancient Greek philosophers saw as the unremitting quest for truth.

Further Readings_____

Barton, S. C. (Ed.) (1999) *Where Shall Wisdom Be Found?* Edinburgh: T & T Clark.
Kekes, J. (1995) *Moral Wisdom and Good Lives*. Ithaca: Cornell University Press.
Lehrer, K. et al. (Eds.) (1996) *Knowledge, Teaching and Wisdom*. Dordrecht: Kluwer Academic Publishers.

What Is Knowledge?

3

Emily Robertson

Knowing is a relationship between a knower and what is known. What is a good description of this relationship? When do our beliefs count as knowledge and when are they merely our beliefs? One traditional account holds that knowledge requires justified true belief. For example, let us suppose that Professor Dunmore claims that social class differences have an effect on educational attainment in the United States. Then, according to the proposed account, Professor Dunmore's belief counts as knowledge only if the claim is true (i.e., it must be the case that social class impacts educational attainment) and she has good reasons for her belief that serve to justify her claim.

If education aims at knowledge, as it seems reasonable to suppose, does the analysis of knowledge as justified true belief square with our educational practices? I think it does. As teachers, we typically want our students to have good reasons for their beliefs. And we do our best to communicate beliefs that are true, although we realize that current understandings may be wrong. We thus encourage students to be open to criticism and revision of their beliefs, even the ones we have taught them, again suggesting that education has an orientation toward truth.

The analysis of knowledge as justified true belief has had many supporters. Yet even among those who accept this account, there have been areas of disagreement. What constitutes having adequate justification for one's beliefs, for example? If a student believes something because the teacher said so, is the student's belief adequately justified? Since a large number of our beliefs are accepted on the testimony of relevant experts, we would seem to know very little if we ourselves had to thoroughly understand the evidence for each of our beliefs. On the other hand, knowing something for oneself seems significantly different from merely taking the word of others. What might constitute good reasons for adopting others' beliefs as one's own? Under what conditions is it reasonable to believe what one reads on the internet, for example?

Another problem for the analysis is that justified true beliefs do not always count as knowledge. (This point was first made in the 1960s by the philosopher Edmund Gettier.) In general, this situation arises when someone has a justified true belief only as a matter of luck. Suppose, for example, that a student forms the belief that his school will be closed next Friday for a teacher workshop because he has heard the principal say so in morning announcements. Since the principal is generally a reliable source for such information, the student justifiably believes that school will be closed on Friday. But unknown to the student, the workshop has been cancelled. Yet on Friday the school *is* closed because of an unexpected snowstorm. In this case, it's only an accident that the student has a justified true belief that the school will be closed and so his belief does not count as knowledge. The evidence the student has for his belief is not connected in the right way to the truth of his belief. This means that the analysis of knowledge as justified true belief is at best not a complete account. And it may mean that some other approach to the analysis of knowledge should be taken.

Another limitation of this analysis is that it applies only to one type of knowledge, knowledge that something is so (sometimes called "propositional knowledge"). A science teacher, for example, may want her students to know that science is empirical and understand what that means. Yet in addition to propositional knowledge, educators are concerned to teach skills and habits that are also candidates for knowledge. A science teacher may want her students to know how to design an experiment or to develop good intellectual habits, a disposition to think critically, for example. The justified true belief analysis does not cover these important types of knowledge.

Some may challenge the requirement of truth or adequacy that this account of knowledge has employed. Constructivist theories of learning, for example, hold that each person constructs his or her own knowledge. Some constructivists argue that different individuals or groups may arrive at conflicting yet equally valid beliefs, all appropriately called 'knowledge.' *Whose* truth, they may ask, is involved in staking a claim to knowledge? Yet however we answer these questions, the analysis still has some purchase. All individuals and groups seek to improve their fund of knowledge. They modify their beliefs in light of new experiences and information in an effort to arrive at beliefs that are more adequate. If we regarded *all* beliefs as equally valid, why would we be interested in learning or education? Knowledge appears to be a particularly valuable form of belief that meets some additional criteria. Exploring the question "What is Knowledge?" is an attempt to discover those criteria.

Furthermore, there are important questions about knowledge that are not answered by the justified true belief account. Is the goal of knowing to have an accurate representation of some portion of reality? Are such representations possible? Can knowledge be objective? What does 'objectivity' mean? Do the concrete and particular features of knowers (their gender or their specific cultural and historical locations, for example) have significance for our understanding of knowledge? What are the limitations of the human capacity for knowledge? How can we best acquire knowledge? The justified true belief analysis does not address these questions.

Finally, this account of knowledge has used examples that focus on individual knowledge. Yet knowledge has a social dimension. The content of the curriculum that schools teach is the result of cognitive activity by communities of inquirers, the scientific community, for example. Individual learners construct their own knowledge using the resources of public bodies of knowledge created by these communities. How such communities operate and the role that particular social and political factors play in their knowledge construction is a subject of much contemporary debate.

Since no one has the relevant evidence for all their beliefs or even a significant portion of them, authority and trust play a major role in individual knowledge construction. We are often in the position of justifying our beliefs by relying on the testimony of experts, as we noted above. The role of authority in shaping our knowledge claims is necessary but also troubling, since it rests on differential power relations. This situation is made more troubling by the fact that differences in expert status may coincide with differences in social, economic, or political power. While there is no simple solution to this situation, a dominant aim of education should be not only to acquire knowledge derived from the achievement of others, but also to learn how to engage in critical dialogue, in give and take with others in our communities of knowing, in the interest of generating more adequate knowledge claims.

Further Readings_____

Adler, J. E. (2003) Knowledge, Truth, and Learning, in Randall Curren (Ed.), *A Companion to the Philosophy of Education.* Oxford: Blackwell: 285-304.

Carr, D. (Ed.) (1998) *Education, Knowledge and Truth: Beyond the Postmodern Impasse.* London: Routledge.

Longino, H. E. (1999) Feminist Epistemology, in John Greco & Ernest Sosa (Eds.), *The Blackwell Guide to Epistemology.* Oxford: Blackwell.

What Is Imagination?

Candace Jesse Stout

On Family Night in the schools, what a teacher expects and what actually happens can be a momentous mismatch. Exchanges about curriculum, learning activities, goals, and student progress are anticipated. Pleasantries from most, reproach from some, punctuate the course of those evenings. But sometimes things move differently. Little epiphanies arise in bright abruptness evoking the need for readjustment by both teacher and visitor. Take the case of Tracey and the silkworm farm. In my early years of teaching, Tracey was a senior in my high school humanities class. He spoke very little, interacted even less, but beyond that silence and lassitude few students I knew were as imaginative as he. On Family Night, students' projects on "The Arts Beyond Medieval Europe" filled our room. Some were predictable; others outstanding. But tucked in a corner through the creator's choice, the *Seeds of the Mulberry Tree* ruled the evening. Delicately balanced between image and text, this miniature diorama was Tracey's interpretation of the secretive Chinese sericulture, before the medieval smuggling of silkworm eggs and mulberry seeds opened the "silk roads" to the West. Through a glittering frame, a kind of ancient Chinese doorway, the viewer encountered a three-dimensional, theatrical scene: rows of modeled trees replete with suspended cocoons of fine, golden fibers, all set in the landscape of rivers, bridges and mist-shrouded hills of sixth century China. Posted at the left were biological data on mulberry trees and the lifecycle of Bombyx mori. On the right were Chinese and Japanese haiku. On seeing the diorama, Tracey's parents were skeptical, their expectations being vociferously and invariably low. As they explored the images and read the text, skepticism morphed to credence, then to gaping amazement and one indelicate but honest question: "Where did *this* come from?" The school buzzers sounded. The parents moved on to the next scheduled class. Their question left unanswered still loiters in my mind.

In one sense, the scenario with the dumbfounded parents was rewarding. Several months before, Tracey had accompanied his father, a professor of agricultural research, to China where they visited a silkworm farm. Outwardly unreflective on his return, the family assumed the teenager's impressions were nil, but those few moments in his brilliant little landscape provoked a new recognition of the seventeen year old boy who inhabited their house. In their burst of intuition, their readjustment of consciousness, Tracey had won some respect.

In another sense, I had my own re-thinking to do. In reflecting on that night and the candor of those parents, I realized how little they understood and how imperceptibly they valued the work of imagination. The glitter, the watercolor hills, the tiny golden bundles, and the poignant Asian poems, I cannot say precisely where these remarkable things come from, but in following Dewey, I believe they are born of a dissonance between an external vision, those outward perceptions of lived experience, and an internal vision, those mental images we nourish in our own interior landscapes. We are presented with an object or a scene, or we undergo an event, or we act in some manner. From our own situated standpoint, we reflect on those experiences, and in the midst of introspection, we envision something new - maybe richer and deeper. On that research trip to China, Tracey ventured beyond the pursuits of the agricultural science in which he and his father were commonly immersed. In the dissonance between the contemporary sericulture and the possibilities that played within his interior view, imagination arose kindling a sensibility more empathic and whole. The reality he was envisaging went beyond a modernized silkworm farm. Steeped in tradition and shrouded in lore, it was the people that he was imagining, their thinking and feeling and acting, their rootedness in a lost and venerable land.

At the end of his travels in China, all unknown to his disappointed parents, Tracey took that ancient world home. Those outward perceptions and those internal reflections settled in and became part of the family of his experiences, germinating and expanding in his mind. And in the generosity that defines an arts and humanities curriculum, in each of his individual research and creative projects, Tracey chose to return to China; he wanted to see more of the people and their past. In those participatory encounters with the arts, he took his imaginative journeys and his interests and sympathies grew. In autumn, he found Chinese haiku, Tu Fu's screech owls in yellowing mulberry trees, and Japanese verses as well – Basho's silkworms sick from too much rain. In winter, he read Italo Calvino's *Invisible Cities* – Marco Polo in the evening garden with the aged Kublai Khan. As our class studied ancient Chinese scrolls, creating ink and watercolor landscapes, Tracey painted an intimate space for himself in the rivers and mountain paths. In April, the diorama was complete, a quiet little testimony to the imaginary nexus where self and insight and other might meet.

After all of my years of teaching, my reading, and my studies, I remember that late evening question and the radiant *Seeds of the Mulberry Tree*. Where do those paintings and poems, those sparkling dioramas come from? They come from the moments, gathered up, of our lives. They emerge from our thinking and feeling and acting, our open-minded reflecting on that question: What if? Invested in all of those artworks, be they poems or paintings or a teenager's creations, are the "what ifs" and "as ifs" of the artists as they consort with their life-world of experience. As the outer and inner worlds meet, imagination plans an excursion, a divergence to an alternate path where we cross the boundaries of our own experience and share in the possibilities of others. If we are open and willing like Tracey, we return from our imaginary wanderings to our own experiential home, bringing with us new appreciation and perspectives which integrate with the whole of our lives. It is imagination that brings the parts together shaping the life we make for ourselves and for the world we envision as a whole.

Further Readings

Dewey, J. (1980) *Art as Experience*. New York: Perigee Books (Originally published in 1934).

Gardner, H. (1993) *Creating Minds*. New York: Basic Books.

Greene, M. (1995) *Releasing the Imagination*. San Francisco: Jossey-Bass.

What Is Authority?

Nicholas C. Burbules

Authority is one of the lynchpin concepts in education. It seems intrinsic to the meaning of teaching that someone can offer expert advice or information, ask questions, give assignments for work or practice, or evaluate what a learner is doing. All of these activities depend on an explicit or implicit consent – or at the very least willing compliance – by that learner. Education may be based in a hierarchical teacher-student relation, or in the reciprocal teaching and learning that takes place among peers or team members, or even in the independent interaction between a learner and a text: but in any of these settings the question of what sustains such consent or compliance can be raised.

For Max Weber, and for later sociologists and social theorists, the bases of such authority needed to be differentiated from *power*. Whereas power was seen as a coercive way of securing compliance, authority was seen as the legitimate form such relations can take, in which compliance is voluntarily (even if reluctantly) given, or in which authority is, in the stronger sense, actively granted and consented to. For Weber, authority can be based on *traditional* grounds (for example, the authority granted to elders in certain cultures); on *charismatic* grounds (for example, the authority granted to a hero or other inspiring and admirable figure); or on *legal-rational* grounds (for example, the authority granted to judges or others who hold a formal institutional role and responsibility). Later theorists have also added *professional expertise* as a basis for legitimate authority (for example, the authority granted to physicians' judgments and opinions). Teaching, it is often argued, partakes of some or all of these bases of legitimate authority.

Foucauldian theorists would not accept the Weberian distinction between power and authority, and would subject even the bases of 'legitimate' authority to critical scrutiny. Given their more expansive conception of power, they would identify the presence of coercive force in even apparently voluntary or consensual relations. Whose interests are served by institutional roles and responsibilities, for instance, or how are popular understandings of professional expertise grounded in manipulative or self-interested turf protection by those groups privileged by such authority?

The notion of teacher authority has also been criticized on other grounds. For radical and critical pedagogues inspired by Paulo Freire, any hierarchical teacher-student relation mirrors the relation of oppressor and oppressed in unequal societies: Freire proposed instead a radically egalitarian pedagogy, where teachers and learners are engaged in a mutually edifying relation in which all might learn from the others. However, as Freire himself came to acknowledge, this does not mean that all teacher authority is corrupting: a critical pedagogue seeking to foster emancipatory learning will still need to rely on some kinds of authority ceded to him or her, even in the effort to motivate and 'empower' the learning of others. Similarly, many feminist theorists in education have struggled with the dilemma of seeing authority as linked to unequal and patriarchal relations, on the one hand, while trying to formulate a distinctively feminine or feminist alternative: one linked to maternal roles or caring relations, for example, or one linked to experiments in de-centering and problematizing authority even in the midst of (inevitable?) authority relations.

Across all of these views, the line between authority and authoritarianism needs to be questioned. At what point might the *presumption* of authority, or the *extension* of legitimate authority into areas where it is not justified, constitute an abuse of authority? Even defenders of legitimate teacher authority need to delimit such a boundary. For more skeptical views, as noted previously, a strict distinction between legitimate authority and authoritarianism cannot be maintained, because all authority is seen as involving coercive elements. For radical critics of schooling, especially during the 1970s and 1980s, schools were seen as havens of authoritarian and inegalitarian relations that belied the commitment of schooling to opportunity for all students. During the later 1980's and to the present, Foucauldian analyses have tended to predominate the critical agenda, focusing less on the disjunction between promise and reality in schooling, and more on the inevitable, if subtle, operations of power in even apparently innocent and consensual interactions.

And yet it seems significant that we are discussing authority *in education*, and not just authority as a general social and institutional phenomenon. Schools, as real institutional settings, certainly can exhibit all the forms of coercion, abuses of authority, or false and exaggerated assertions of authority that we might find in any other institutional settings (courts, say, or coaches of athletic teams). Nor are such authoritarian shortcomings absent in even more altruistic and informal settings, such as families. A certain realism about the imperfection of human relations seems apt here.

Nevertheless, when we think about education as an endeavor, the activity of any type of teaching – even that among peers or relative equals – seems to require something like authority, and the willing grant of authority from learner to teacher. This type of relation seems intrinsic to the very idea of education in a way that it is not necessarily intrinsic to many other types of social interaction (friendship, for example). Hence it is always appropriate to inquire into what legitimates such authority, either in principle or in practice.

At the same time the context of education seems to put certain constraints on the exercise of authority that are not typical of other social or institutional contexts. For one thing, the exercise of a teacher's authority seems to involve many activities that do not seem intrinsically subject to authoritarianism: listening, encouraging, guiding, and helping, for example. These activities can be overly romanticized, and each can foster its own kinds of asymmetries. But they present a different face of authority from the more immediately apparent teaching activities of offering expert advice or information, asking questions, giving assignments, and evaluating learner performance. Furthermore, the idea of *reciprocity*, of learning while teaching, seems more a feature of the teacher-learner relation than it is to, say, the relation of a judge to a defendant in court. Finally, and perhaps most significantly, authority in education is in some sense *self-undermining*: the goal of authority in teaching, generally speaking, is to encourage learners to raise questions with the teacher, to subject authority to scrutiny even where its basic legitimacy might be accepted; and ultimately, to make teacher authority itself redundant and unnecessary.

Further Readings_____

Burbules, N. C. (1995) Authority and the Tragic Dimension of Teaching, in J. Garrison & A. G. Rud (Eds.), *The Educational Conversation: Closing the Gap*. New York: SUNY Press, 29-40.

Nyberg D. & Farber, P. (1986) Authority in Education, *Teachers College Record* 88 (1): 4-14 (This issue also contains a number of responses to Nyberg and Farber).

Pace, J. L. (2003) Revisiting Classroom Authority: Theory and Ideology Meet Practice, *Teachers College Record* 105 (8): 1559-1585.

What Is Open-mindedness?

William Hare

Open-mindedness involves being critically receptive to new ideas especially when they seem wildly improbable, contrary to what we might wish to be true, or potentially threatening to apparently secure and cherished beliefs. It tends to flourish when supported by other traits such as intellectual humility, where we acknowledge our liability to error, and intellectual courage, where we are not afraid to consider the possibility that a certain idea might be true or worth pursuing. Open-mindedness replaces dogmatic certainty, which makes further reflection and inquiry appear pointless, with a determination to consider what is to be said for and against the matter in question without bias or prejudice in so far as that is possible. An open-minded person is ready to entertain an unusual point of view, to admit that an unwelcome conclusion indeed follows, and to concede that a position presently held needs to be revised, but only if a critical review of relevant considerations indicates that the ideas in question have merit.

It is clear from this that the attitude of open-mindedness, despite familiar accounts, cannot be adequately characterized as the ready acceptance of ideas. Such readiness might indicate mere credulity or capriciousness. An open-minded person will not take an idea seriously unless it is judged to be supported to some degree by relevant evidence and argument. That is what is meant by critical receptiveness. Confusion about open-mindedness, and corresponding doubts about its value, result from neglecting the factor of critical appraisal that is a necessary feature of genuine open-mindedness. Such neglect means that open-mindedness is often erroneously linked with relativism, abandonment of principles, general skepticism, inability to stick with a line of inquiry, and reluctance to come to a conclusion. These theories, however, ignore the fact that open-mindedness is perfectly compatible with firm belief and decisive action. Complete confidence in a particular belief or decision can co-exist with an awareness that we make mistakes; and recognition of our fallibility makes open-mindedness, even where we are most sure, both possible and desirable. What matters is that one's beliefs remain subject to revision in the light of experience and reflection.

Open-mindedness is enormously difficult, however, not simply because even relatively tolerant societies impose constraints on what can be freely examined in teaching or elsewhere, but because we ourselves create obstacles to open-minded reflection. We take it too much for granted that we are open-minded without noticing the various ways in which we allow our prejudices to distort and limit our own consideration of new ideas. We may also lack the courage to face unfamiliar and unwelcome ideas and consequently dismiss them without the attention they deserve; and we may draw back from the uncertainty and ambiguity that open-mindedness requires us to live with.

Open-mindedness is generally desirable not because it necessarily or invariably leads to the formation of true beliefs or morally appropriate decisions, but because searching for and assessing what is to be said for and against a certain conclusion is more reliable than guesswork, conventional wisdom, and wishful thinking. We are entitled to be more confident about our position if we have considered the case for and against it and if we continue to pay serious attention to emerging perspectives and interpretations. There may, of course, be occasions when we judge that it would be wiser to avoid a certain set of ideas than to expose ourselves to fanatical propaganda; we do not demonstrate our open-mindedness by keeping up with the literature from the Ku Klux Klan.

To espouse the ideal of open-mindedness in education is not to reject the importance of communicating established knowledge, useful skills, and familiar moral principles; indeed, it is not possible to think in an open-minded way about various possibilities, in science or in ethics, unless one is well informed and familiar with current ideas, techniques, and values. It does mean, however, that knowledge, skills and principles cannot be taught as absolute and beyond question. An education that incorporates a commitment to open-mindedness promotes a climate of free and honest inquiry and stands opposed to all forms of indoctrination, manipulation, and propaganda; it encourages the attempt to identify and examine assumptions and prejudices that tend to remain hidden; and it recognizes that what we confidently teach and learn today may well need revision in the future. Open-mindedness in education is reflected in an emphasis on fostering in people the inclination to approach new ideas intelligently and independently, and to revisit what they have previously learned.

These ideals entail significant conclusions about the manner in which teachers need to go about their work. Open-mindedness does not mean that teachers must avoid revealing or arguing for their own opinions on controversial matters, but it does mean that teachers must seek in every way to convey to their students the idea that such opinions are simply the ones they themselves presently hold, that they stand or fall depending on the weight of evidence and argument, that other teachers and experts might well hold different views, and that students are expected to come to their own conclusions. The challenge is to communicate all of this without suggesting that one conclusion is no better than another. Open-minded teachers invite and encourage students to develop their own ideas in a thoughtful way, to criticize the opinions they encounter in textbooks or from teachers, and they cultivate an atmosphere in the classroom in which a spirit of open inquiry predominates, and where ideas are advanced tentatively and provisionally. Teachers need to set an example of open-mindedness in the way in which they themselves seem curious about ideas, are ready to admit to having made a mistake, present their views as open for discussion, remain willing to entertain an alternative view put forward by a student, and are anxious to avoid steering the discussion towards a predetermined conclusion. All of this will contribute to the teacher being seen by the students as someone who sees himself or herself as still having much to learn.

Further Readings_____

Bramall, S. (2000) Opening up Open-mindedness, *Educational Theory* 50 (2): 201-12.

Hare, W. (1985) *In Defence of Open-mindedness.* Montreal: McGill-Queen's University Press.

Hare. W. (Ed.) (2003) *Journal of Thought* 38, (2). Special issue on Open-mindedness and Education.

What Is Caring?

Nel Noddings

'Care' and 'caring' are words that appear in ordinary language with a variety of meanings. Sometimes care is associated with worries and burdens; we have 'cares.' Sometimes it is used synonymously with care-giving or caretaking: we are charged with the care of a person, place, or object. Teachers often think of caring as an attitude of concern, as in, "I really care about my students!" Some interpret this concern mistakenly as a warm, fuzzy sort of attitude. Others, equally mistaken, believe that caring as concern requires them to force students to do whatever the school requires. From this perspective, a caring teacher makes students do what is good for them. In ethical thought, however, caring involves much more than a warm attitude or feeling, and it avoids coercion.

An ethic of care emphasizes relation and response. It uses 'caring' to refer primarily to relations in which the efforts of a carer are received as caring by the recipient of those efforts. Without the recognition of the cared-for, a relation cannot be described as caring – no matter how hard the carer has tried to care. We may credit the carer with trying to care, but something is still amiss.

In everyday life, we know how important the recognition of the cared-for is in caring relations. An infant contributes to the parent-child relation by smiling, wriggling, and cuddling. Patients respond to the efforts of physicians by expressing relief. Students respond to their teachers by pursuing projects and tasks of learning. All of these responses contribute to the satisfaction of carers. Without such responses, it is difficult to maintain our efforts to care, and we may suffer burnout. In addition, the response of the cared-for is part of what the carer receives in a new round of attention; it is vital to the maintenance of a caring relation.

What characterizes the consciousness of carers? What describes how we feel and act when we care? Caring requires, first of all, that a carer be attentive to the cared-for. In caring, we listen non-selectively to the cared-for to determine, as nearly as we can, what the cared-for needs – what she or he is feeling. As we listen, we are affected; we feel something akin to what the cared-for is feeling. We put ourselves in a posture of vulnerability, and we may feel a hurt or fear similar to that experienced by the cared-for. We also feel our motive energy flowing toward the needs of the other. Usually, we want to help in meeting this need but, sometimes, we may want to persuade the cared-for that the need expressed is really not in his or her best interest. The task is more difficult in the latter event but, in both cases, we want to respond in a way that will establish or maintain a caring relation.

Receptive attention and motivational displacement characterize the consciousness of carers, but they do not tell us what to do. Now we have to think, discuss, and plan. We have to decide what to do on the basis of what the cared-for has expressed, on our evaluation of the need expressed, and on our capacity to respond. Teachers who are superbly well-prepared are in a better position to respond effectively to the expressed needs of students than are those less well-prepared. If I am well-prepared not only in, say, mathematics but also in a broad range of humanistic studies, I may be able to suggest projects, tasks, and alternative assessments that will allow a student who hates mathematics to succeed in my math course despite his fear and hatred. If I am not so well-prepared, I may insist that the student meet the pre-specified objectives. I simply would not know enough to suggest valuable alternatives that might meet both the student's needs and the course requirements. For this reason, in a number of my books and essays, I have claimed that caring implies competence. Teachers must become more and more competent in order to meet the legitimate needs of their students.

But suppose a student expresses a need of which I cannot approve? Suppose, for example, that a student wants to drop the courses required for college entrance. A process of dialogue and negotiation must be instituted.

Perhaps the student will convince me that, since he does not plan on going to college, he really doesn't need these courses. Then I have to encourage continued dialogue so that I can be sure that he has chosen wisely and that he will be adequately prepared for the goal he has chosen. Perhaps, however, the student does want to go to college but is just bored, fearful, and discouraged. Then my task is to support and help him by negotiating generously between his present needs and the needs we identify with his long-range goal of going to college. This is work that requires getting to know the student and "staying with" him through this difficult period.

As mentioned earlier, teachers often make the mistake of supposing that caring is best demonstrated by forcing students to do what the school requires. This attitude is encouraged in schools today by the great emphasis on universal standards and assessment by standardized tests. Sometimes a form of "tough love" is even accepted by students as genuine caring. Students will say of a teacher, "She really cares; she makes us do the work." An ethic of care casts doubt on this claim to care through coercion. Is this the sort of life that we want for our students – that they will do whatever the teacher or boss insists upon? Or should we encourage them to accept some responsibility for their own growth? Caring teachers invite students to share responsibility for both the choice of educational objectives and the ways in which they will be assessed. In this process of negotiation, teachers learn something of what their students are undergoing, and students have an opportunity to reflect on their own goals and make commitments accordingly.

This way of teaching may seem difficult, and indeed it does require a high level of competence. But it is enormously rewarding, because students become engaged with material that they have had a hand in choosing. The result should be both the joys of genuine caring relations and a commitment to continued educational growth.

Further Readings

Noddings, N. (2003) *Caring: A Feminine Approach to Ethics and Moral Education*, 2nd edition. Berkeley: University of California Press.

Noddings, N. (2005) *The Challenge to Care in Schools*, 2nd edition. New York: Teachers College Press.

Noddings, N. (2005) Caring and Competence, in Gary Griffen (Ed.), *The Education of Teachers*. Chicago: National Society for the Study of Education: 205-220.

What Is Leadership?

James Ryan

Academics, practitioners and the general public increasingly see leadership as the key to making organizations, institutions and communities better places. But few can agree on what kind of leadership strategies work best. More striking though is that even fewer can concur on the meaning of leadership. At bottom, leadership is a contested term; advocates of various positions vie with others to have their views or meanings accepted. Despite the contested nature of the meaning of leadership, certain views have prevailed over time. Recently though, newer perspectives on leadership have emerged and are challenging the more traditional approaches. These struggles are taking place over what many would see as the basic elements of leadership – (1) the place or role of individuals, (2) the nature of relationships among people, and (3) the ends for which leadership is organized.

Contests over the meaning of leadership are important because the outcome will dictate the manner in which people in organizations and communities govern or manage themselves. While they may be commonplace – some may say trivial – in academia, such contests are not exclusive to this antiseptic world. They inevitably spill out into the real world of practice; the way in which people envision leadership will dictate how it is put into practice in their institutions. Ultimately, leadership is about power – who gets to decide what for whom. If the prevailing view is that leadership resides within individuals, then it will be individual people who will exercise their power to influence practice. On the other hand, if the accepted view is that leadership is a collective enterprise, then power will not reside exclusively or largely in the hands of a single individual, but with a group of people. Views of leadership will also dictate the direction (hierarchical or horizontal) in which power will be exercised and the ends to which power is employed.

The dominant perspective sees leadership as residing in individuals. It has a long history. For many years, political scientists have studied the lives of legendary people – kings, presidents, initiators of social movements – individuals who were able to use their remarkable personal gifts to change the course of history. Many organizational theorists and management scholars have also operated under the assumption that leadership resides with individuals. Endowed with the power associated with personal qualities or organizational position, it is individuals – leaders – who practise what we have come to understand as leadership. Such a view, however, is increasingly being challenged. One alternate approach, for example, circulates the idea that leadership is a collective rather than an individual practice. Another related view that departs even more radically from the latter is that leadership is a collective *process*. Proponents of this position emphasize the process dimension, while promoting the idea that leadership power emerges from people working together in enduring and practised ways.

Struggles are also occurring over the type of relationship that proponents envision among people. The dominant perspective views leadership in terms of a hierarchy. In these schemes certain individuals (leaders) assume power over others by virtue of their personal qualities or their organizational position. Adherents to this perspective believe that these hierarchies are necessary to compensate for most of humanity's inability to look after itself in an increasingly uncertain and threatening world and for organizational members who are not capable of, or cannot be trusted to do, the work for which they are responsible. The role of gifted or officially appointed leaders then becomes one of employing their power to force, guide, motivate, inspire and/or elevate the less willing, able and motivated to do what is expected of them. Exponents of other perspectives, however, hold a more positive view of humanity. They reject the idea that all people are inherently unequal, believing instead that they are capable of looking after their own affairs and responsible enough to carry out tasks associated with their and others' welfare. As a consequence, they campaign for equitable and non-hierarchical or horizontal relationships among people in organizations and in the wider community. They contend that leadership need not be associated with a position or always with certain supposedly gifted individuals, but that everyone can and should have the power to influence what happens in their own ways and times. In this sense power is not employed by one or more people to control others, but used as a resource to work for collective interests.

Contests also occur over the ends for which leadership activities are organized. On the one hand, the more traditional conservative approaches advocate for the achievement of comparatively narrow organization goals. Other than efficiency and productivity such ends remain pretty much undefined, unique to the respective institutions. The role of the leaders then is to use their power to motivate employees to work as hard as they can to achieve such goals, which generally – but not always – are designed to support the status quo. This approach has been challenged by perspectives that focus on broader and explicitly stated social goals and visions. For example, a commonly stated goal is the achievement of social justice. Those who subscribe to this position see leadership as the means for destabilizing the status quo and with it, unjust practices like racism, sexism, classism and homophobia. Here the power of leadership is used to empower the powerless.

There are in principle an infinite number of approaches to leadership. Those interested in leadership have the option of selecting not just from two positions – the dominant and challenger – but from many versions that reside somewhere in between prototypes. The various options include, among many others, moral leadership, participative leadership, managerial leadership, democratic leadership, transactional leadership, leadership for the differently-abled, student leadership, parent/community leadership, emancipatory leadership, shared leadership, distributed leadership, instructional leadership, transformational leadership, and teacher leadership. The many versions that fall under these banners are not typically just hierarchical or horizontal, but often display elements of both. To complicate the terrain even more, leadership perspectives often combine more traditional perspectives with more recent non-dominant approaches. It is not uncommon to see individualistic and hierarchical leadership combined with a quest for social justice, contradictions notwithstanding. Just as leadership approaches are in principle infinite in number, so too are the power relationships that characterize the practices associated with them.

Ultimately, leadership is about power. It is about how we govern and are governed in our organizations and communities, and about what kind of world we want these governance practices to uphold. This is why it is so important that we understand the leadership perspectives that we favour. For the view of, or meaning we attribute to leadership will determine who makes decisions that count, whose interests these decisions favour, and what our organizations and communities will inevitably look like.

Further Readings_____

Ryan, J. (2003) *Leading Diverse Schools.* Dordrecht: Kluwer.
Smyth, J. (Ed.) (1989) *Critical Perspectives on Educational Leadership.* London: Falmer.
Yukl , G. (2001) *Leadership in Organizations.* 5th edition. Toronto: Prentice Hall.

What Is Educational Theory?

Paul Standish

All research begins with values. This is true of qualitative and quantitative educational research. It is true across the range of scientific research, even where this is understood in positivist terms. It is true without exception. This is the case because all research begins with something that matters. Why else would it be undertaken in the first place? And mattering is a matter of values.

Ethics is the science of value and one of the most central elements of philosophy. If we bridle at the term 'science', let us just say that it is enquiry into the nature of value. And so, ethics is relevant to all research at its starting point. In empirical research it concerns the values at the beginning of enquiry (the topic, the questions asked, what is to count as data . . .), as well as those inherent in any discussion of results. In educational policy and practice also values are there at the start. Without values the idea of a practice makes no sense. Values are definitely not just something you 'add'.

Courses in the ethics of research have become mandatory for trainee educational researchers, and publications on these matters are plentiful. But their concern, typically informed by codes of practice and increasingly mindful of the law, is normally confined to methodological matters – to do with consent, confidentiality, and the like. All this is important, and yet an exclusive emphasis on such matters has a reductive effect: for researchers in education, as in other fields, this is what ethics has come to mean. Concentrating on the middle, empirical phase of the work, this is less than half the story. It deflects attention from the values that condition enquiry, surreptitiously implying that they are unproblematic. Gruff practicality takes over: what is really needed is to show what works - what evidence best supports policy and grounds practice.

Where does this leave educational theory? What, in any case, is meant by 'theory'? A quick response will contrast theory with practice, associating the former with bookish, highly general, abstract enquiry. That's all very well in theory, the familiar response runs, but will it work in practice? To be involved in practice is to do something; to do theory is not. In consequence, theorists will seem insulated from the real world of educational practice, the value of their work routinely called into question. But this theory-practice contrast does not stand up to scrutiny. A first reason is that to engage in theory is itself to be involved in a practice; it is, contrary to the above, to *do* something. A second concerns confusion over the relationship between the ends of theory and of practice – that is, between bookish and discursive enquiry, on the one hand, and teaching at the chalk-face or empirical data-gathering, on the other. In Aristotle's terms, the *natural* sciences are theoretical in that their purpose is the advancement of understanding; ethics and politics, in contrast, are *practical* sciences, the purpose of which is better action. It follows that to study Aristotle's *Nicomachean Ethics* in this way - bookish perhaps, but with the discursive engagement it should prompt - is itself part of this practical science. Not that the theoretical and practical sciences are tidily separated: to *act better* we need a sound *understanding* of what human nature and the socio-political conditions of our action are like. Acting well requires realism, and being realistic involves a complex blend of practical and theoretical wisdom.

To refer to such (bookish) enquiry as educational *theory* is, then, something of a misnomer. Educational theory is properly so named to the extent that it is concerned only with the understanding of practice and not with its improvement. Academic research into politics or art, for example, is often dedicated not to the improvement of practice but simply to increased understanding of salient aspects of our social world. Why should there not be educational research along similar lines? In general, however, and for a variety of reasons, the work to which researchers in education departments are committed is concerned directly or indirectly with improvement in practice. The institutional reasons for this are plain enough. Students in university departments of education are, for the most part, educational practitioners; the courses they take are usually designed to develop professional expertise. Much research, therefore, takes off from concerns with what that expertise consists in and with the conditions in which it is best exercised. Moreover, to the extent that educational researchers are employed as teachers in universities, they are directly involved in the professional activity that is otherwise their object of study. In this respect they have an exceptional position within the academy.

Just as any ethics of research confined to methodology must be woefully inadequate, so enquiry into professional practice that does not foreground the pervasive nature of questions of value will be severely deficient. It will fail to sensitize practitioners to the practical reason they need. If we ask how this practical reason is to become more fully present in practice, then it seems reasonably clear that this will not in the main be through empirical research. Enquiry into these matters needs to be philosophical, ethics being, as we saw, one of the central elements in philosophy. And given that all research begins with questions of value, other branches of philosophy will also be conditioned in this way – not least in their commitment to truth. Epistemology, so obviously relevant to education, is simply incoherent without assumptions and judgments about the value of knowledge. Ethics, we see again, is pervasive.

This is not to make a case exclusively for philosophy: in recent decades other forms of enquiry also have been sidelined in favor of supposedly more practical study and research – one thinks of history and sociology, as well as comparative education. Nor is it to advocate philosophical approaches of a narrow disciplinary kind. It is to accept the breadth of the ways in which enquiry can fruitfully take place, albeit that any systematic study of ethics is bound in some degree to be philosophical.

The mantle of 'theory' can be accepted to the extent that the addressing of questions of value that is advocated here will perforce involve greater *understanding*. Teachers are not technical operatives who do not need to understand the operations they are performing. The understanding they need is internally related to practice. The teacher with practical wisdom is someone whose knowledge is manifest in the doing. Her activity is in-formed by this better understanding, whether or not this is articulated.

But this is not, finally, a matter of theory applied. To see things in such terms is to resuscitate a picture of the theory-practice relation that has dogged the philosophy of education, amongst both advocates and detractors. The point is not to pass on, *de haut en bas*, an understanding of the ethics of education that the humble practitioner can put into operation. It is to enable the practitioner to think better about what she is doing, and in this to improve her practice. This may indeed involve thinking about ideas in books such as the *Nicomachean Ethics*. Call this theory if you will.

Further Readings_____

Blake, N., Smeyers, P., Smith, R., & Standish, P. (2003) *The Blackwell Guide to the Philosophy of Education*. Oxford: Blackwell.

Dunne, J., & Hogan, P. (Eds.) (2003) Education and Practice: Upholding the Integrity of Teaching and Learning, Special Issue, *Journal of Philosophy of Education* 37 (2).

Hirst, P. H., & Carr, W. (2005) Philosophy and Education: a Symposium, *Journal of Philosophy of Education* 39 (4).

What Is Professionalism?

Shirley R. Steinberg

It is many times easier to answer a question by looking at the non-answers. In doing this, we are able to read between the lines, and to find the hidden meanings that can speak directly to us. What is professionalism? I would prefer to ask what professionalism *is not*. By isolating the issues and themes that do not belong in a professional educator's *space/life-world*, I believe we will begin to be able to discover our own professionalism.

Unfortunately, educators are up against an elitist academic world that insists that education is somehow a vocation that should possibly be conducted out of the academy. Many of us fight daily to insist on the respect and acknowledgement that belongs with the profession of teaching children and youth. Often educators relent to an embarrassed stance that allows other disciplines to trounce upon education as a second-class career. Ironically, this is the only discipline that prepares the entire population to enter any and all professions. When educational professionals become empowered with the knowledge of their essential place in the world, the academy will begin to listen and respond. We are responsible for instilling within ourselves the fact that we are professionals. Only then can we demand that we are professionals.

What professionalism isn't: It isn't deskilled. In fact, it isn't a skill at all. It is an art. It includes interpersonal genius, scholarly genius, empathetic genius, a demand for inquiry, diversity, and passion. Professionalism is not measurable, it cannot be quantified. One cannot put professionalism into a scale, taxonomy, or rubric and evaluate it. It does not need labels, titles, or certifications in order to exist. Professionalism exists because the student who is nurtured by an educational professional reflects and rigorously demonstrates knowledge and practice.

Professionalism is not easy, it is not pre-packaged, and it is not predictable. Educational professionalism requires the ability to research, create, and revise different notions and concepts. It can not be purchased by a district or region and imposed upon a group by an administrator. I am reminded of the hundreds of teachers who used to pack into a Florida stadium to become *better teachers*. School districts became obsessed with the Madelaine Hunter methods of lesson preparation. Schools purchased thousands of dollars of video tapes, teachers spent hours viewing the tapes and learning Hunter's seven step lesson plan. When Hunter and her promoters realized the millions of dollars they were bringing in, they began to enlarge the inservice to become stadiumized. Teachers would leave the assemblies with tee shirts proclaiming that they had been *Hunterized.* This type of practice possibly reveals why the academy has little respect for educators. An educational professional is not anti-intellectual, and opposes those that attempt to reduce knowledge into rationally compartmentalized videos, websites and scripted lesson plans.

Professionalism is not arrogant. As educators we should demand a humility that requires self-reflection. The ability to read and understand ourselves should be central to both our pedagogy and personal development.

By deconstructing our own actions and thoughts, we are able to re-visit our own world and acknowledge what needs to be done for improvement and professional success. This self-study sets an example to our students that we, as teaching professionals, are consistently attempting to better ourselves. Self-reflective actions, by nature, avoid arrogance.

Professionalism is not objective. Every particle, bit of knowledge, and historical event is subject to the interpretation of both the teacher and the student. As professionals it is important to articulate our subjectivities and allow for the articulation of the subjectivities of others. Professionalism is not apolitical. By its very existence, teaching is a political act. A professional educator should not seek to replicate the status quo, but to continually improve upon it. Pedagogical professionals are committed citizens of the world, attempting to integrate a vision of social justice within every strand of their relationship with students.

Professionals do not indoctrinate. We do not use our students to pour our ideological agendas through. Professional educators attempt to enlighten, to facilitate empowerment, so that students are able to choose and identify the ideologies that they are most comfortable with. We walk a fine line between our own ideals and ethics, and the ability to teach yet not insist that our students adopt *our* way as the only way.

An educator who wishes to be a professional does not expect to stay safe. She or he takes risks. A teacher often must make the choice to present two curricula: the official, and the un-official. The ability to critically read the educational environment and political climate may result in having to create a subversive set of knowledges in order to maintain a commitment to being the best teacher/citizen possible. The ability to read the school, the administration, and the community must be combined with the knowledge of what the students *need* to know in order to learn and thrive in society.

Professionalism is not 9-5. It is not summers off, and lots of vacation days. A teacher does not leave the job in the school and return home without somehow being affected by the day's events and the students. An awareness of the conditions of the community, school, and students' environments is essential to being a teacher. Acknowledgement of socio-economic differences, ethnicities, and one's own positionality is part of our being. Who is it that we are teaching? How are we different? How are we the same? These questions must be articulated and tentatively answered as we continue to grow with our students. As we strive to learn who they are, we must equally allow them to understand who we are.

An educational professional is not disrespectful of other educators. This may seem a simple notion, but can often be the most difficult. While we should feel comfortable with critique, we need to understand that the value of critique comes from a desire to improve and assist, not to denigrate or to destroy. Our students and colleagues watch us closely, and in order to be seen as professionals, we need to treat our peers as professionals.

There will be a day when educators do not have to claw our way out of the proverbial barrel in order to be recognized as the professionals we are. The responsibility is overwhelming, and we have much to do.

Further Readings_____

Freire, P. (1998) *Teachers as Cultural Workers: Letters to Those that Dare Teach.* Boulder, Co.: Westview Press.

Kincheloe, J. (1992) *Teachers as Researchers: Qualitative Paths to Empowerment.* Philadelphia: RoutledgeFalmer.

Schon, D. (1983) *The Reflective Practitioner: How Professionals Think in Action.* New York: Basic Books.

What Is Teacher Education?

Sophie Haroutunian-Gordon

The phrase "teacher education" typically refers to a program of study undertaken by those preparing to teach in the pre-kindergarten, elementary, and secondary schools. In America, the program may be offered as part of a baccalaureate, master's degree, or "fifth-year" program, or as an "alternative" approach to teacher education.

In a traditional program, students might complete: courses in foundations of education (history, philosophy, psychology); methods of teaching (e.g., English, science, mathematics, social studies); observation in one or more schools; student teaching under the direction of an experienced (mentor) teacher; courses on curricular topics (e.g., technology, curriculum design, particular instructional approaches) as well as issues in teaching (e.g., multicultural, legal, assessment). In some cases, students complete a research project related to teaching or education more broadly conceived.

An "alternative" approach might ask people with baccalaureate or higher degrees to complete a four-to-eight week summer session orientation and then begin an appointment as a full-time teacher. The novice may or may not have a mentor, but regardless, he/she has primary responsibility for the students. Coursework is emphasized to a lesser extent than in a traditional program.

According to the National Commission on Teaching and America's Future, 46% of all teachers leave the classroom within 5 years. The National Center for Education Statistics, published August 2004, stated that 32.5% of those who left the classroom did so for reasons of dissatisfaction with the job.   That figure is higher than those who left in order to retire (29%), to raise a family (16.5%), or to earn more money and benefits (19%).

It is not hard to imagine why many teachers leave their classrooms out of dissatisfaction: drop-out rates range from 20 to 60 % in urban high schools; high-stakes testing forces teachers to devote more and more class time to test preparation; districts, under pressure to meet certain standards of student achievement, tie teachers to "scripted" curricula that allow little choice about how to present the subject matter and engage students in learning. Here you have three sources of discontent, and I but scratch the surface.

D.C. Lortie states in *Schoolteacher: A Sociological Study* (1975), "It is of great importance for teachers to feel that they have 'reached' their students – the core rewards are tied to that perception. Other sources of satisfaction (e.g., private scholarly activities, relationships with adults) pale in comparison with teachers' exchanges with students and the feeling that the students have learned." Lortie's research reaffirmed that teaching is, after all, grounded in the humane bonds formed between student and teacher. Perhaps we lose many teachers because life in schools has become intolerably inhumane.

Let me explain what I mean by that statement. In schools where drop-out rates are 20-60 %, relations between many students and teachers are arrested, for there can be no relation if one party is absent. In schools that lose funding because students score poorly on standardized tests, teachers are forced to use their skills and talents to help students score better, which may shift attention away from the many needs, talents, and interests that each student brings to the study of the discipline. If the teacher is required to follow a "script" and behave only as directed, he/she may need to ignore knowledge, creativity, personal interests, skills, and talents – in short, much of the self – or lose the job. Perhaps such living deserves abandonment.

The greatest challenge facing teacher education today is to help teachers live a fully human life in the classroom under the constraints of high student drop-out, high stakes testing, and a curriculum driven by meaningless or inappropriate standards that puts a pall on creativity. Effective teacher education, be it traditional or alternative, will help teachers to keep thinking, keep growing, and help students learn how academic disciplines make life meaningful. It will provide resources that energize rather than innervate. It will habituate the teacher to develop those resources despite pressures to abandon them.

And what are those resources to be cultivated and cherished by the teacher? First is the ability and will to question until the point of doubt is clear – to question both the subject matter and the learning of the students. For example, if students are not doing well in science, what, exactly, is the problem? Clarifying the question requires interpreting texts so as to distinguish between that which is to be accepted and that which is unclear. The texts may include documents specified by the curriculum, data sets, student work samples, student reflections on their experiences, and conversations between student and teacher.

Second, teachers need to develop the ability to listen to the perspectives that conflict with their beliefs. Only by listening, and listening in various ways to the student, the curricular texts, and others, can the teacher identify the precise point of doubt and get help resolving it. If the ideas that they hear challenge their understanding and convictions, the way may be opened to new, productive thinking about resolution(s) of the question.

Finally, teachers should learn to reflect – to ponder the relation between the question and what they hear (through written or spoken word). Those who question, listen, and consider what they hear in relation to what they wish to know may keep thinking and growing: they may use what they hear to find and address queries about the subject matter and the needs of the students, doing so in the context of serious academic pursuits. Such teachers may develop the personal relations and satisfactions that they seek in entering the teaching profession.

Now, how might teacher educators help to cultivate these resources in teachers? They might, for example, offer opportunities to prepare for, lead, and reflect upon what I and the Great Books Foundation call "interpretive discussion," that is, discussion about the meaning of texts. Teachers prepare for such discussions by writing questions about things they do not understand in a text – questions to which the teacher educator responds by asking for clarification, suggesting possible meanings for ambiguous phrases, and directing the writer to passages which, if interpreted, may have implications for resolving the dilemma. Those questions may challenge the writer's thinking and help clarify the point of doubt.

Once the question is clear, and the discussion has taken place, the teacher educator may ask the teacher/leader to identify the issue of concern to the group and reflect upon the discussion-leading patterns that helped the issue to form. Such patterns include: repeating back to participants their comments and questions; identifying similarities and differences in people's views; asking participants to clarify their meaning; and asking for textual evidence. Reflecting upon the patterns that they followed may help teachers/leaders to engage discussants in forming questions they wish to resolve. Cultivating such questions through discussion builds human bonds.

Further Readings_____

Dewey, J. (1916). *Democracy and Education*. New York: Free Press.

Haroutunian-Gordon, S. (1991). *Turning the Soul: Teaching through Conversation in the High School*. Chicago: The University of Chicago Press.

Meier, D. (1995). *The Power of their Ideas: Lessons for America from a Small School in Harlem*. Boston: Beacon Press.

What Is Postmodernism?
(How Is Postmodernism?)

Maureen Ford

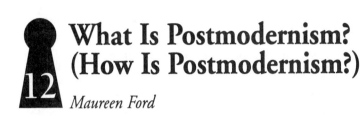

> Picture a building in which all the systems necessary
> for maintenance, operation and structural integrity
> are constructed in plain view – so as to be
> visible to the building's inhabitants.
>
> ❦
>
> Can you see the ghosts in the shadows?
> Estimate the costs of construction?
>
> ❦
>
> What makes it possible to associate skyscrapers
> with civilization?
>
> ❦
>
> Now fashion language as such a building.
>
> ❦
>
> Fashion science, and history, and social justice
> as such buildings.

There are many varying ways to tell the story of modernity but for the moment I want to relate an account associated with philosophers and statespeople at least since the time of Immanuel Kant ("What is Enlightenment?" ca. 1784). Modernity, according to this account, is an age defined by its social and philosophical characteristics. It is an age in which 'humanity' comes into its maturity through the exercise of Reason. In what some have called a "Copernican revolution" Kant recast the world with a humanist centre by setting human perception (rather than the Divine or the Sovereign) as the ground of understanding. Thus, modernity presents itself as a historical turning point; governance by Reason becomes associated with liberation, freedom, autonomy, and good government.

Education has pride of place in this story of modernity as it is through education that governance by Reason is made possible. By developing the capacity of people to think critically (rationally) about the nature of things and events, education generates the conditions for social progress. Though over-simplified as told here, this is a commonly told story. We usually associate schooling with the skills, attitudes, passions and virtues of critical thinking. We have inherited a story of modernity called "The Enlightenment," and have characterized it with the themes of individualism, meritocracy, and positivism (the belief that objective knowledge gives us access to a 'real' world).

Postmodernism, to the extent that it can be represented as a story at all, is a story juxtaposed to modernity, neither 'after' nor 'against,' but, rather, set alongside and in tension with modernity. Postmodernism is:

- a story of doubt regarding the dominant *meta-narratives* of progress associated with modernity;
- a story of contestation regarding the privileging of human consciousness as the prime mover of understanding;
- a story that troubles assumptions of transparency with respect to language, subjectivity, and the presence of an objective world to human consciousness.

Postmodern scholars (postmoderns) invite us to partake in processes that reveal the structures that enable us to generate understanding or meaning, and then consider how those structures sometimes limit what we can think about and how we can act.

Postmodernity is many stories – structuralisms, poststructuralisms, postcolonialisms, anti-colonialisms, psychoanalyses, feminisms, queer theories, anti-racisms, globalizations and antiglobalizations. Honouring the ethos of postmodernity requires that we pay attention to the differences as well as to the commonalities in these accounts. Postmoderns turn thought on its side. Not quite upside down – but not quite business as usual either – because we want to disrupt the ways our thoughts and speech are typically carried out.

One group of postmoderns works from a position that focuses on linguistic *difference* – the recognition that the structure of language limits a speaker or writer's options about what to say and how it might be said. They study the effects of gaps in our capacity to use language to say what we mean. Their work can help us to notice slippage or play in language-use that demonstrates freedom we might otherwise fail to take up. By paying attention to the effects that poststructuralists map, for instance, teachers can notice that identifying successful school performances immediately confronts all those who don't "fit the mould" of success with identification as "school failures." Acting on this linguistic insight, teachers might resist trying to find better definitions of success and to embrace efforts to find multiple ways of enacting and sharing successes.

Another group of postmoderns, queer theorists, pays a different kind of attention to difference. Their work begins in contexts where questions about sexuality and embodiment are raised (for instance mapping how school campuses continue to be amongst the most oppressively conventional and unsafe places for many folks who live outside sexual 'norms'). Ultimately, though, queer theorists are concerned about processes of normalization wherever they generate practices of exclusion or violence. Queer theorists question (queer) the processes of racialized or dis/abling norms. Queer theorists unpack the scripts invoked by, and within, school contexts such as those that prioritize tasks associated with administrative accountability (standardized testing, classroom management, "covering the curriculum,") over tasks associated with student engagement (learning from student resistance, inclusion and/or anti-racism).

Postmodern stories decry the pseudo-universalism of conventional modernist stories of progress (the "discovery of the Americas" or the 'democratization' of Iraq). They are political even as they contest the terms by which political relations and power are investigated. Postmoderns resist articulating analyses of centre and margin (mainstream vs. special needs, citizens vs. refugees) *as if these can be stable positions.* Postmodern stories regarding political tensions and contestations make room for speaking and acting in opposition to racism or sexism as well as forms of resistance that reconstruct old and new patterns of separation, confinement and exile (feminist accounts that pay too little attention to the diversity of political relations shaping the school experience of girls, boys, and the intersexed).

These stories are not always construed most effectively as stories; sometimes strategies of juxtaposition or parody better convey, invoke, or trouble, taken-for-granted frames of reference. From postmodern perspectives, dependence on the capacity to generate better, more complete, more authoritative arguments as the means by which to oppose dominating narratives, appears not only inadequate, it becomes suspect. Such dependence invites deconstruction. This is the point of changing the question "what is postmodernity," with its goal of definitiveness, to the question "how is postmodernity" with its attention to performativity (i.e., identifying effects of linguistic strategies, such as the acts of naming or defining, as proactive rather than passive).

The pride of place schools occupy in modernity ensures their significance for postmodern activity. School emphases on getting the right answer, and on developing the competencies (docility) that promote associations of agency – the capacity to act – with knowing the right answer, contribute to the narrowing of ways we might act and think differently. Here, the point of opposition is, again, not to deploy a new version of "what is the right thing to do". It is to pay attention to our desires for activities and competencies – learning, engaging, creating, playing – that broaden the chances for human and planetary sustenance.

Further Readings_____

Lyotard, J-F. 1997 (1979) *The Postmodern Condition: A Report on Knowledge.* Trans. Geoff Bennington and Brian Massumi. Minneapolis: University of Minnesota Press.

Britzman, D. (2003) *Practice Makes Practice: A Critical Study of Learning to Teach.* Albany: State University of New York Press.

Peters, M. (1998) *Naming the Multiple: Poststructuralism and Education.* Westport & London: Bergin & Garvey.

What Is Curriculum?

William F. Pinar

The organizational and intellectual center of education, curriculum, is defined variously as 1) a course; a regular course of study or training, as at a school or university (OED); 2) a course, especially a specified fixed course of study, as in a school or college, as one leading to a degree; the whole body of courses offered in an educational institution, or by a department thereof (Webster's, 2nd edition); 3) all of the experiences children have under the guidance of teachers; 4) all educational opportunities provided by the school; 5) the plans or programs for all experiences which the learner encounters under the auspices of the school, including extracurricular activities.

From a comparison of these dictionary definitions (the first two) with those formulated by scholars who study curriculum (the last three), it is obvious that the dictionary definitions are deemed too narrow, too simple, incomplete. John Dewey accepted the customary definition, implying that curriculum is knowledge which, organized ordinarily along subject matter lines, is to be mastered by students. Dewey did see a problem with the customary definition, however; it stipulated a divide between intellectual content and students' experience. For Dewey, intellectual content and students' experience were two limits of a single educative process.

In his definition of curriculum, Franklin Bobbitt included 'out-of-school' experiences, introducing a distinction between 'directed' and 'undirected' experience, the latter referring to 'out-of-school' experience. The curriculum of 'out-of-school' experience enabled curriculum scholars to argue that various institutions, ranging from the church, mosque, and temple to the media and business, from day-care centers to the family itself, have curricula and that the school curriculum often challenges these other curricula. For example, certain fundamentalist Christian parents express reservations regarding the "secular humanism" of the public school curriculum, alleging that it undermines the 'curriculum' of Christianity.

Twenty years after Bobbitt's 1918 work, the definition of curriculum expanded further to include unwanted consequences of schooling, including the hidden curriculum, the unstudied curriculum, and the unwritten curriculum. Additionally, there have been definitions of the curriculum that emphasize what is not offered in the official curriculum, i.e. the so-called 'null' curriculum as well as the 'out-of-school' curriculum. The concept of the hidden curriculum suggests that this unofficial curriculum may be ideological, communicating political messages subliminally. The concept of the curriculum as lived enables scholars to emphasize students' and teachers' experience of the curriculum as planned.

A variegated and shifting concept, curriculum is a highly symbolic concept; it is what the older generation chooses to tell (and not tell) the younger generation. So understood, the curriculum is understood to be historical, political, racial, gendered, phenomenological, autobiographical, aesthetic, theological, and international. Curriculum is the intellectual site on which the generations struggle to define themselves and the world.

Curriculum is an extraordinarily complicated conversation. Stated institutionally, the school curriculum is a formalized, often abstract, version of conversation, a term usually invoked to refer to open-ended, sometimes personal, often interest-driven events in which persons encounter each other. That the school curriculum has become so formalized and distant from the everyday sense of conversation is an indication of its institutionalization and its bureaucratization. Instead of employing others' conversations to enrich their own with students, teachers are required to 'instruct' students to participate in others' - i.e. textbook authors' - conversations, employing others' terms to others' ends. In such a conception, school curriculum is identified with the academic disciplines as they themselves have been institutionalized and bureaucratized over the past one hundred years. Over the past thirty years the U.S. curriculum field has attempted "to take back" curriculum from the bureaucrats, to make the curriculum field itself a conversation, and in so doing, work to understand curriculum.

The point of the school curriculum is, scholars agree, not only to train students as specialists in the academic disciplines. The point of school curriculum is not only to produce accomplished test-takers, so that, for instance, U.S. scores on standardized tests compare favorably to Japanese or German scores. The point of the school curriculum is not to produce efficient and docile employees for business. The point of the school curriculum is to goad citizens into caring for ourselves and our fellow human beings, to help us think and act with intelligence, knowledge, sensitivity, and courage in both the public sphere – as citizens aspiring to establish a democratic society – and in the private sphere, as individuals committed to other individuals.

Once the point of the curriculum is shifted away from the institutional, economic, and political goals of others, it becomes clear that the curriculum is a historical event in itself. That is, as soon as we take hold of the curriculum as an opportunity for ourselves, as citizens, as persons, we realize that curriculum changes as we reflect on it, engage in its study, and act in response to it, toward the realization of our civic ideals and private dreams. Curriculum ceases to be a thing, and it is more than a process. It becomes a verb, an action, a social practice, a private meaning, and a public hope. Curriculum is not just the site of our labor, it becomes the product of our labor, changing as we are changed by it.

Curriculum studies is the interdisciplinary specialization within the broad academic field of education that conducts research on the curriculum. Within curriculum studies are further specializations, among them curriculum theory and history. The former focuses on the intellectual traditions that have shaped public and scholarly debates over the curriculum; the latter focuses on the educational experience, including as it is structured in the school curriculum as planned, as enacted, as lived. In addition to curriculum theory and history, curriculum studies has included scholarly attention understanding curriculum politically, in gendered terms, phenomenologically, in postmodern terms, autobiographically and biographically, aesthetically, theologically, institutionally, and internationally. Professional associations such as the American Association for the Advancement of Curriculum Studies (**http://aaacs.info**) and the International Association for the Advancement of Curriculum Studies (**www.iaacs.org**) support the scholarly study of curriculum.

Further Readings_____

Jackson, P. (Ed.) (1992) *Handbook of Research on Curriculum*. New York: Macmillan.

Pinar, W. F., Reynolds, W. M., Slattery, P., & Taubman, P. M. (1995) *Understanding Curriculum*. New York: Peter Lang.

Pinar, W. F. (Ed.) (2003) *International Handbook of Curriculum Research*. Mahwah, N.J.: Lawrence Erlbaum.

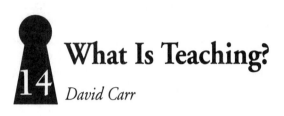

What Is Teaching?

14   *David Carr*

In addressing the question of what teaching is, we first need to be clear what precisely the question is asking. Is it (for example) asking what kind of *activity* teaching is, or what sort of *occupation* it is? These senses of teaching are clearly different, since one may teach without being (by occupation) a teacher; but connected, in so far as (most) teachers do teach. Either question is complex, however, since different notions of teaching as occupation may be suggested by different views of the activity of teaching (and vice versa). Following some examination of the activity of teaching, however, we shall proceed to explore various implications for views of teaching as an occupation.

What, then, of the activity of teaching? Does it, for example, require the acquisition of knowledge, ability or skill? If so, what is such expertise and how is it acquired? In recent times, teaching has come to be regarded as a scientifically grounded technology: on this view, the capacities required for effective teaching are skills determined by empirical research into learning. Professional teacher training is seen in turn as a matter of initiation into such skills or 'competencies'. Still, to whatever extent teaching might sometimes be improved by such research, any exclusively empiricist conception of teaching expertise seems suspect.

First, it seems unlikely that good teachers are so mainly by virtue of research based knowledge. Teaching has often been effective without benefit of such knowledge – and it seems odd to suppose that modern research might suddenly 'discover' a hitherto unknown teaching skill. Second, it seems that teaching skills are not readily amenable to scientific generalization: they are highly context sensitive, and what works in one situation may not so work in another. Thirdly, it may be quite inappropriate to think of some of the qualities required by good teachers – such as wisdom, patience and imagination – as 'skills'.

Still, to doubt that teaching is entirely reducible to research-based skills is not to deny that it may involve *skill*. Unlike the general research-based skills of technicians, the skills of artists are highly flexible and context specific – and, indeed, teaching has often been regarded as more like a 'performance art'. On this view, good teachers are not so much the mechanical followers of pre-prescribed routines, but creative pedagogical 'artists': whereas technical skill (e.g.. auto-repair) 'goes by the book', good teaching requires imaginative (perhaps 'thespian') expression and invention.

But the 'artistic' view is also problematic. First, much school learning is fairly routine or otherwise constrained, and there are obvious limits to creative and imaginative pedagogical expression in the classroom. Secondly, the artistic view may seem dangerously subjective or idiosyncratic, and insufficiently accountable to principled professional constraints. Indeed, thirdly, it seems clear that 'artistic' teachers may be charismatic and imaginative without necessarily doing much very effective teaching – if their lessons are longer on style or presentation than actual substance.

Perhaps, however, one could regard good teaching as some hybrid of the technical *and* the artistic. Good teachers might be *both* masters of research-based pedagogical technique, *and* capable of personally charismatic, creative and imaginative engagement. That said, one can also think of those whom might fit this profile of highly charismatic and technically effective instructors of others (such as Hitler) whom one might hesitate to describe as 'good teachers'. Hence, insofar as education is a matter of *improving* people in some substantial normative sense, good teaching would seem to be a *moral* as well as a technical or artistic matter.

Conceived thus, good teaching would appear to have diverse moral implications. First, if pupils have rights not to be abused, indoctrinated or exploited, and teachers have obligations to respect such rights, there will be ethical constraints on the professional practice of teachers. Secondly, teachers and schools have often been held accountable for the explicit moral and social improvement of young people as well as for their academic or vocational instruction. Thirdly, however, this suggests that good teachers need to be certain kinds of *persons*, possessed of *virtues* – such as fairness, integrity and patience – that are not obviously reducible to skills.

Arguably, then, the portrait of the good teacher is a complex mosaic of technical, personal and moral characteristics. Good teachers may need certain technical skills, but they also need to be creative and inspirational. But, as well as attracting the interests of pupils, they need to create an appropriate *moral* classroom climate and to develop the virtues of moral exemplars. For purposes of professional teacher preparation, it also needs appreciating that these diverse qualities are also variously acquired: one does not become an effective organiser as one becomes interesting – and becoming patient is a different matter again.

How one conceives the occupational character of teaching may depend on how one balances these diverse elements in the portrait of the good teacher, or to which of these elements one gives highest priority. Teachers have formerly been compared to various other occupational groups: if the value transmission aspects of education are emphasised, teaching may be compared to religious ministry; if the caring dimensions are stressed (as in early years education), teachers may be compared with nurses; if the remedial or social service aspects are emphasised teachers may be likened to social workers.

More recent discussions of the professional status of teachers have focused on yet other comparisons: while some have regarded teachers – by virtue of the high social and moral purpose of education – as members of professions in the same sense as doctors and lawyers, others have opposed tendencies to 'deprofessionalization' implicit in a 'tradesman' conception of teachers as operators of routine skills prescribed by others. In addition, recent 'market' conceptions of education seem also to have cast teachers and head-teachers more in the roles of business managers and salespersons.

Whilst one should not ignore the real enough tensions between all such analogies, the grains of truth in all of these comparisons nevertheless indicate that teaching is an occupation of considerable complexity that has yet to receive the close analysis it truly merits.

Further Readings_____

Carr, D. (2000) *Professionalism and Ethical Issues in Teaching*. London: Routledge.
Hare, W. (1993) *What Makes a Good Teacher*. London, ON: Althouse Press.
Passmore, J. (1980) *The Philosophy of Teaching*. London: Duckworth.

What Is Inquiry?

Heesoon Bai

Generally, there are two kinds of learning: one that prepares a person for tangible, reducible, measurable, definite, and predictable outcomes, like the exam questions in school; and another kind that 'prepares' a person for the uncertain, ambiguous, and unpredictable aspects of life. Learning that 2 + 2 = 4, along with a billion other 'facts' and know-how's that children and adults learn in schools, belongs to the first kind. Life, however, is full of the immeasurable, irreducible, uncertain, and unpredictable not only because the world is simply a bewilderingly complex place; but also because when humans face the life-world, they don't just see trees, people, food on the table, money in the bank, and so on, but *see* and *feel* such strange and nebulous things as beauty, love and compassion, joys and sorrows, fear and security, fairness, injustice, and so on. These *qualities* belong to the realm of the *meta-physical*, in the sense of going beyond the tangible, quantifiable, measurable, and even effable. This meta-physical is, however, the dimension of personal meaning and insight, and there is nothing vague and inconsequential about it. Lack of the meaningful can sink us in misery, and kill our spirit, if not our body.

School learning is predominantly about the first kind of learning. We stuff our students with a billion bits of information and skills. Know this; know that; do this; do that. You will be tested to see how much you've retained of what we have taught you. The questions we want you to handle have definite and correct answers. We won't ask you questions that have no pre-given or fixed answers, and you need not ask them, either. After decades of this kind of learning, no wonder that we become anxious and distressed about life's uncertainty, complexity, unpredictability, and mystery. We become attached to the power of predictability and control, certainty of beliefs, security of facts, and strength of morals. But life refuses to be reduced to our expectations. In the end, we have to learn to navigate in the sea of the metaphysical and work with life's uncertainty and complexity. Inquiry is this kind of navigation.

In inquiry, we ask questions for the creative possibility of seeing things differently for more enriched, novel, vital, or deeper meanings. Inquiry is our quest for meaning or sense-making, value, purpose, perspective, and awareness. When we realize that all the facts in the world do not add up to reveal more adequate or satisfactory meanings, purposes, and values that enthuse and empower one's life, we begin to ask different questions: Are there different ways I can conceptualize and apprehend aspects of life and the world, self and other, than how I took things to be previously when I was presented with them as 'normal,' 'natural,' 'inevitable,' 'factual,' 'objective,' and 'true'? Inquiry starts with the suspicion and realization that things do not have to appear the way they do; that their appearance has all to do with my implicit or explicit choice to interpret, evaluate, and assign meanings to them even without changing their factual content. In this sense, the realization of one's power of thinking and feeling precedes the practice of inquiry. Thus, if we want our students to undertake inquiry, we first have to help them realize their own power. Needless to say, entrenchment in learning devoted to predictability and control, as is the case in much of our school learning, enfeebles such power.

Open-ended and creative as it is, inquiry is not a practice of "dreaming up anything" and "anything goes." Inquiry is purposeful, requires various intellectual and psychological skills, and is both process and achievement-oriented. As well, it is not something that happens just "inside one's head." Inquiry is in fact most effectively pursued as a group's dialogical activity. This is because the most valuable aspect of inquiry is gaining *perspectives*, which is facilitated by a group of individuals exchanging their perceptions of things, showing and explaining how they see the given matter. Being able to see a notion, an issue, a situation, a person, or what have you, from a variety of angles, against many different conceptual and psychological backgrounds and for particular objectives, trains one to be creative, resourceful, flexible, and fluid. These are the kinds of intellectual and emotional qualities required for the practice of inquiry.

Another point worth noting is that inquiry is not just a discursive practice. While clarification and analysis of concepts, evaluation of arguments, belief revision, and the like can all be part of inquiry, much more is involved besides this discursive element. We get into inquiry because of our desire to see and understand differently, with better insight and creative possibilities of interaction, the particular situation and people that one encounters in one's life, and one's own reactions to them. In other words, inquiry is not an abstract exercise but a living practice. Given this, the most important element in inquiry is what the inquirer brings to the process of inquiry: alert and expansive consciousness, sensitivity and receptivity to people and situations, the ability to feel authentically and strongly, the capacity for sustained investigation, creative impulses, imaginative capacities for trying out different 'realities,' and vitality and enthusiasm. It is well to remember that an inquiry is no longer a living inquiry when the inquirer has abstracted his or her subjectivity out of the content and the process of the inquiry.

In this limited space, I can only touch on how best to conduct an inquiry. This being a *living inquiry*, the best place to start it is wherever one finds oneself existentially. One looks inwardly into one's own thoughts and feelings, while facing the world, noting how one reacts with conditioned thought and feeling responses. Usually we are too busy reacting that we do not stop to reflect and examine our response. Inquiry starts at this point of stop. From this place of stop, we question the necessity of "the way things are," and address the possibility of seeing the world and the self differently and hence relating to the world differently. *"What if I were to. . .?"*

Further Readings_____

Hadot, P. (1995) *Philosophy as a Way of Life.* Oxford: Blackwell.

Nozick, R. (1989) *The Examined Life.* New York: Simon & Schuster.

Solomon, R. (1999) *The Joy of Philosophy.* Oxford: Oxford University Press.

What Is Constructivism?

Barbara J. Thayer-Bacon

I was an elementary teacher for many years, and I am the mother of four children. I have spent a lot of time working with children. Even as a university professor, I still spend time in schools and design research studies that give me reasons to be with kids in classrooms. I learn so much from them! The children in my elementary Montessori classroom got me thinking about how they learn to think. My classroom curriculum did not follow the public school curriculum, and yet my students, who were diverse in ability levels, consistently scored 2-3 grade levels above the norm on the standardized achievement tests I had to give them. I first thought that they must be learning how to be good critical thinkers and they were reasoning their way through the tests and choosing the most logical answers. But, when I looked around my classroom and considered all that was going on, critical thinking did not seem to capture much of what happened each day in class. Absolutely, the children were developing good reasoning skills, but also so much more. They were learning good relational and communication skills, and they were learning to rely on their imagination, intuition, and emotions to help them think, not just logical, analytical skills associated with critical thinking. Thus began my efforts to develop a description of what my students learned in our classroom, what I called "constructive thinking."

I did not know at the time of my adopting that term that there were many people in educational psychology and related fields of study who were working on *constructivism* and that constructivism was having a notable impact on teaching methods, especially in science and math. As a philosopher of education, I was already exposed to the constructivist idea that knowledge is something human beings create in a dialogical relationship with others, for that idea has a long history in philosophy and can be traced back to Socrates in ancient Greece. My inspiration for constructivism came from "constructive knowing" in Belenky et al., *Women's Ways of Knowing*, and is therefore located within feminist scholarship. Their description of knowing as involving both personal knowledge (the inner, intuitive voice) and expert knowledge (the voice of reason) resonated with me. I needed a concept that recognized that the students in my classroom were not just learning expert, public knowledge, what they were reading in books or hearing from me, but they were also using their own personal knowledge to help them think. I wanted to stress the impossibility of separating knowledge, the object, from knowers, as subjects.

I also wanted to stress the impossibility of separating individual knowers, the self, from others who influence and contribute to our thinking, our social community. My classroom was not a traditional classroom where children sat in individual desks and worked independently on their assignments, while I sat at my desk overseeing their work. Our room was a space with tables for working with others and desks for working alone, and rug areas where one could set out a mat and work on their own or with others. As a teacher, I did not have a desk; I had a clipboard that I carried around as I moved to various places in the room. Our room had a lot of flexibility and the boundaries between individuals and others were very porous. I began to see our classroom as a community of learners, and the metaphor of "a quilting bee" came to mind as richly describing our space.

A quilting bee emphasizes that constructive thinking is something we do with others. We may go off by ourselves to puzzle over a problem, but we are social beings who grow up with the help and loving care of others and those others influence our own thinking. And then there are all the others we come in contact with and interact with through our conversations, readings, even our television viewing. A quilting bee emphasizes that we, the quilters, are actively involved in constructing quilts of knowledge within a social context, even as we sew our own, unique quilt squares.

A quilting bee positions people in the role of doing the constructing, making us active participants in the quilting process. *We* are constructing quilts of knowledge. We do not discover the quilts out there in the world, or in ourselves, we make them together. And, the 'we' is pluralistic and multicultural; quilts are made by males and females of varying ages and abilities all over the world, in a variety of forms, using diverse designs, with a creative array of material, colors, and textures. The flexibility and diversity of a quilting bee helps us think about constructive thinking in terms of recognizing that we are diverse thinkers as well as helping us recognize the diverse products we produce and the diverse ways we go about producing them. A quilting bee metaphor offered me a way to recognize and value the many activities my various students did in our classroom, not just the reading and writing work, but also the physical and artistic activities that were a part of our daily curriculum.

What about the tools used for quilting, for constructively thinking? They are simple and adaptive, and yet essential. The material we use to make quilts represents our ideas that we use to help us construct quilts of knowledge. We cannot constructively think without ideas. The colors of the material represent our emotional feelings and the designs and texture represent our imagination. Our tools include a needle and thread of some kind, and scissors, straight pins and a ruler or template of some kind. The needle and thread represent our intuition, helping us move through our ideas and find a way to pull them together. Our critical thinking skills, our reasoning, are our scissors, rulers, and straight pins we use to help us cut out the ideas and fit them together; they are the tools we use to measure our ideas and judge them for their quality. I want to argue that we use all of these to help us constructively think, and they should all be highly valued. As you look around *your* classroom, I hope you find that the image of quilters coming together to construct quilts of knowledge will help you notice and value all that is going on.

Further Readings

Belenky, M., Clinchy, B., Goldberger, N. & Tarule, J. (1986) *Women's Ways of Knowing*. New York: Basic Books.

Thayer-Bacon, B. (2000) *Transforming Critical Thinking: Thinking Constructively*. New York: Teachers College Press.

Thayer-Bacon, B. with Bacon, C. (1998) *Philosophy Applied to Education: Nurturing a Democratic Community in the Classroom*. Upper Saddle River, N.J.: Prentice Hall.

What Is Indoctrination?

Charlene Tan

Indoctrination is commonly regarded as antithetical to education or some educational ideals such as rationality, autonomy or open-mindedness. No teacher in his or her right mind would exclaim proudly that he or she enjoys indoctrinating the students. Similarly, any parent who desires his or her child to be indoctrinated will meet with much castigation. However, it is interesting to note that the etymological meaning of indoctrination simply means 'instruction', and 'indoctrination' and 'education' have at times been used interchangeably in the past. But by the second half of the twentieth century, indoctrination had acquired a distinctly derogatory connotation and is now used pejoratively.

Indoctrination is best understood as the paralysis of one's intellectual capacity, characterized by the inability to justify one's beliefs and consider alternatives. An indoctrinated person is incapacitated intellectually in three ways. Firstly, the person holds to beliefs or values without any good reasons or rational justification. Secondly, an indoctrinated person not only lacks good reasons for holding to certain beliefs; he or she is unable to justify these beliefs. In other words, such a person is incapable of critically inquiring into the worthiness of the beliefs. The third aspect is closed-mindedness or a dogmatic style of belief; this is evidenced by the inability and unwillingness of the indoctrinated person to consider alternatives. Indoctrination is reprehensible because an indoctrinated person is no longer capable of thinking independently. In extreme cases, an indoctrinated person is easily manipulated by others to inflict harm on oneself and others. For example, in the notorious Washington sniper case, one person who was believed to be indoctrinated was prepared to lie, go to jail or even die for his indoctrinator. It has also been reported that suicide bombers are indoctrinated to view killing themselves and their enemies as an act of martyrdom, not suicide or murder.

The fear of indoctrination has led some teachers to avoid teaching any beliefs or values in a directive way. The assumption is that indoctrination is necessarily avoided when students are allowed to question everything, discover values for themselves, and make their own decisions. There are two reasons why this assumption is flawed. Firstly, it overlooks the fact that the tools of inquiry used by students when they are exposed to a myriad of views are ideologically biased. While indoctrination is commonly associated with objectionable teachings such as those taught by the suicide bombers, it can also take place in a liberal democratic form of education. In such a case, the students are indoctrinated into the beliefs and values of pluralistic, democratic liberalism without having any good reasons to support these beliefs and values. Lacking the ability to justify these beliefs and values, their minds are impervious to alternative belief systems which exist in non-liberal societies. Secondly, the fact that the students, especially young children, are taught a substantive set of beliefs and values without any rational basis does not entail that indoctrination has taken place. Indoctrination does not refer to the mere lack of rational justification or evidence for one's beliefs. For example, the multiplication tables are learnt by rote in the classroom without any justification given, yet we would not say that the students are indoctrinated. Likewise, all of us accept beliefs such as the sun will rise tomorrow without a prior investigation of the evidence but we are certainly not victims of indoctrination.

To have a clearer understanding of indoctrination, it is important to understand the process of belief inculcation. All children need to be introduced to some form of initial worldview or primary culture before they can make sense of the world. Certain desirable habits of conduct and positive character traits such as ability in moral reasoning need to be inculcated. This process of belief inculcation involves a non-rational process. Any talk about the development of moral reasoning and personal autonomy can only come after the child has learnt certain moral principles or virtues in a non-rational manner. As mentioned, indoctrination refers to the paralysis of one's intellectual capacity, characterized by the absence and inability to hold to well-grounded beliefs and to consider alternatives. If teachers continue to deprive the child of the reasons for certain moral actions, and stifle the child's moral autonomy to the effect that the child remains uncritical and is unable to imagine alternatives, then indoctrination has taken place.

To avoid indoctrination, educators need to ensure that there is a framework for the appreciation and evaluation of different beliefs and values among people, and the capacity to establish one's own beliefs and values. One such useful framework has been suggested by Ronald Laura and Michael Leahy. Firstly, it is essential for children in Western societies to be initiated into the values and beliefs of liberalism, and be able to give reasons to justify these beliefs and values. However, they should also understand and accept the fact that different values and beliefs are exalted in other countries. For example, teachers could point out that the concept of the individual is subsumed under the collectivistic conception of the community in countries like Japan. The child is then encouraged to reason about such differences and examine the foundations for such differences. In this case, the child needs to comprehend that different countries stress different values due to a nexus of historical, cultural, political and social factors. This sets the background for the child to critically evaluate these factors and form his or her own conclusions. Finally, the child should be encouraged to critique the tools of inquiry used in the thinking process. For example, he or she should examine any ideological bias in and limitations of critical thinking. The overall aim is to equip the child with the intellectual capacity to consider the reasons for one's beliefs and values, be aware of the alternatives, and be willing to revise or change one's views. This form of education does not indoctrinate – it moulds the child and draws out his or her potential, which is what education is all about.

Further Readings

Harvey, W. C. (1997) Liberal Indoctrination and the Problem of Community, *Synthese* 111 (1): 115-130.

Laura, S. R. & Leahy, M. (1989) Religious Upbringing and Rational Autonomy, *Journal of Philosophy of Education* 23 (2): 253-265.

Snook, I. (Ed.) (1972) *Concepts of Indoctrination: Philosophical Essays.* London: Routledge & Kegan Paul.

What Is Critical Thinking?

18

Sharon Bailin

The idea of critical thinking is certainly not new. Philosophers as far back as Socrates have viewed critical thinking as central to the very idea of education, and most, if not all of the goals of our educational systems call for individuals who are effective thinkers. Critical thinking is centrally involved in learning basic academic skills, in becoming a citizen in a democratic society, in becoming a responsible and competent worker, and in making wise life choices.

What is critical thinking? Thinking critically involves attempting to make a reasoned judgment about what it would be sensible or reasonable to believe or do in a given situation. It is not a question of reaching a pre-determined right answer, but it does have to do with the quality of the reasoning which supports the judgment. Thus what makes thinking 'critical' as opposed to 'uncritical' is that it involves fulfilling appropriate standards of good thinking. Conceptualizing critical thinking in terms of engaging in particular processes (e.g., analysing, problem-solving, decision-making) does not necessarily capture the 'critical' element in thinking since any process could be engaged in carelessly, superficially, or unreflectively – in other words, in an uncritical manner. Rather, the term 'critical thinking' emphasizes the quality of thinking required in order to analyse appropriately, solve problems competently, or reach sound decisions. It is, then, the adherence to certain criteria which is the defining characteristic of critical thinking.

What do we need to know, then, in order to foster critical thinking? First, critical thinking always takes place in response to a particular task or problematic situation (critical challenge), e.g., some question, problem, issue, decision, inquiry, or doubt which requires or prompts thinking. Second, critical thinking is contextual. It is best thought of not as a set of generic skills or strategies which can be applied to any situation regardless of the variables. Rather, it takes place in particular contexts and the context determines what qualifies as a sensible or reasonable response to a particular challenge. Third, in order to deal with a critical challenge, the thinker must bring to bear a complex array of understandings or intellectual resources. The precise resources needed for any challenge will depend on the particular context. These intellectual resources include:

1. *Criteria for Judgment*
   Since critical thinking is centrally concerned with the quality of thinking, a knowledge of the principles which govern quality thinking and judgment is at the heart of critical thinking. These include criteria of argumentation and logic, criteria for practical deliberation, and criteria governing inquiry and justification in particular areas of study. Examples of some common criteria for judgment are accuracy, coherence, clarity, feasibility, fairness, plausibility, and originality. Some criteria have a wide range of application across many contexts (e.g., the principles of logic) and some are specific to specific areas (e.g., the criteria which govern the evaluation of historical evidence).

2. *Critical Concepts or Vocabulary*
   These are the concepts that facilitate thinking and judgment in particular areas by marking certain distinctions or picking out certain aspects which are central to the area. Some common critical concepts are cause and effect; premise and conclusion; inference and assumption; necessary and sufficient condition; bias; point of view. Some concepts have a wide range of application (e.g., premise and conclusion) and some concepts are specific to specific areas (e.g., aesthetic balance; axiom).

3. *Habits of Mind*
   These are the attitudes or values important for critical thinking. Knowing and being able to apply relevant criteria will be of little significance if one does not have a commitment to rational inquiry and the habits of mind which go along with this. These include: open-mindedness, fair-mindedness, independent-mindedness, an inquiring and critical attitude, a respect for high quality products and performances, and an intellectual work ethic.

4. *Background Knowledge*

   This is the information about the topic that is required for thoughtful reflection. The particular background knowledge needed will depend on the particular problem and context.

5. *Strategies or Heuristics*

   Although critical thinking is not simply a matter of following certain procedures or steps, certain strategies may be useful when thinking through a problem (e.g., making a list of pros and cons; talking through a problem with another person; using models, drawings or symbols to simplify a problem).

One of the implications of the preceding account is that critical thinking should be developed in context. The following are some suggestions:

1. *Embed critical challenges in the teaching of the curriculum:*

   Find ways to restructure aspects of the curriculum to focus on problems, issues or inquiries. These critical challenges should require students to make reasoned judgments and not simply involve recall or guessing. There must be plausible alternative responses.

2. *Teach the tools:*

   One cannot assume that students will acquire all the relevant resources on their own. Thus we must introduce them to the range of tools required for the tasks we want them to address and provide opportunities for their development.

3. *Build a community of thinkers:*

   Critical thinking needs to be pervasive throughout the curriculum and the classroom. It is crucially important to foster a classroom climate which nurtures and reinforces critical thinking through the following means:

   i.   Embed critical thinking into classroom expectations by expecting students to make up their own minds, provide reasons and support their conclusions, clarify and qualify comments, seriously consider other perspectives, treat classmates with respect even when they disagree.

ii. Incorporate critical thinking into classroom routines and assignments by regularly using critical thinking vocabulary; scrutinizing textbooks and newspaper articles for inaccuracy, bias, stereotyping etc.; having students explore and defend issues from other perspectives; providing ongoing opportunities to engage in critical and co-operative dialogue.

iii. Teacher modeling of critical attributes by being willing to provide reasons for decisions and actions, attempting to base conclusions on careful and fair consideration of all sides, and being a co-investigator rather than an expert.

iv. Use questioning techniques which go beyond recall, probe for clarification, reasons and evidence, consequences and implications, and invite reasoned judgments.

v. Reward critical thinking in the evaluation of student work.

Further Readings_____

Bailin, S., Case, R., Coombs, J. R. & Daniels, L. B. (1999) Conceptualizing Critical Thinking, *Journal of Curriculum Studies* 31 (3): 285-302.

Ennis, R. H. (1996) *Critical Thinking.* Upper Saddle River, N. J.: Prentice-Hall.

Siegel, H. (1988) *Educating Reason: Rationality, Critical Thinking and Education.* New York: Routledge.

What Is Discussion?

David Bridges

"Let's discuss the matter" is a social and conversational move full of all sorts of significance. In a situation of conflict it can signal a willingness to sit down and find a more peaceable resolution to the dispute; in a business context a readiness to do business; in a decision making context an interest in hearing different points of view and arriving at a conclusion on the basis of argument or consensus; in an educational context a readiness to engage student reflection and opinion and not just a determination to impose the teacher's view as the right answer. Discussion, properly understood, implies and carries with it a whole moral culture as well as some underlying principles about the way that knowledge is developed. This is why discussion has historically been seen as such a central component of social practices deemed democratic; and this is why the use of discussion in the classroom is often seen as an especially democratic form of pedagogy.

Or so I have argued and so I continue to hold. I need, however, to show a little more of the thinking which lies behind this view. First, a little bit of conceptual analysis: what do we look for in order to acknowledge that some talk going on among a group of people is a 'discussion'? I suggest that there are three main requirements.

1. You can't have a discussion unless *different points of view are being put forward on a subject*. You can discuss a topic as an individual (I often introduce my lectures as a discussion) but this similarly implies an interest in putting forward and examining different perspectives, evidence or argument and weighing the pros and cons of a case.

2. You can't have a discussion unless there is some *reasonable level of readiness among participants not merely to listen to what is being said but to give it*

respectful attention, to be responsive to it, to allow (in principle at least) their own views to be changed by what others contribute. You can kill discussion by refusing to give this sort of respectful attention to someone else, by refusing to listen, as easily as by refusing to say anything.

3. You can't just 'discuss' or have a discussion – *you have to discuss something and for a purpose which is something to do with developing your understanding, knowledge or judgment* on the matter which is under discussion. There is in discussion (and unlike conversation which may just be a form of social play) a certain seriousness, purposiveness and attachment to (broadly speaking) an epistemological project of improving understanding.

This, in short, is my account of what it is to discuss. It already carries some important messages for the conditions which are necessary if discussion is to be a vehicle for learning and teaching in the classroom. Notably (and corresponding to the three points above):

1. You have to develop the means to ensure that a variety of opinion is being put forward – initially perhaps by having resources which provide such variety, but also by creating an atmosphere in which divergence of opinion is valued rather than discouraged. This means that teachers have to stop playing the game of inviting discussion while providing or guiding the group towards what they see to be the right answer. It also means that teachers have to build students' confidence in contributing their views (and overcome some of the cultural as well as personal barriers to such expression) and positively to reduce the pressures for consensus and conformity that the student group itself will exercise on its members.

2. You have to develop a climate in which this diversity of opinion is listened to respectfully and attentively and in which people feel able publicly to shift in their opinion. Any social authority which the teacher can carry in the classroom has to be directed to this purpose: to protecting diversity of opinion; to encouraging people to weigh evidence and argument rather than authority (including the teacher's academic authority); to valuing the movement of opinion on the basis of evidence

and argument and acknowledging this as a success rather than as a defeat.

3. You have to render the discussion purposive, to ensure (as far as possible) that the resources are available which will enable participants to be properly informed (or that they know where to go to find the information they may require) and to focus on the epistemological requirements of the task in hand, the kinds of things which might count as relevant evidence, reasons or argument in coming to a view on the matter under discussion.

The teacher's role becomes thus very much a procedural one. He or she needs to exercise procedural authority on the social processes of discussion and also on the epistemological requirements. In the process students themselves learn new roles as participants in a process which carries social requirements about how they relate to each other and to the teacher and epistemological requirements about how they come to an opinion.

The practice of discussion thus carries with it a moral culture which is both at some minimal level a condition of being able to discuss at all and which is developed more strongly through experience in discussion. It *requires* and it *cultivates* a measure of peaceableness, orderliness, reasonableness, mutual respect, truthfulness and equality – even if these principles are not necessarily fully observed in all instances. In so far as these principles reflect democratic values and processes, then initiation into the practices of discussion provide an important foundation for education for democratic citizenship itself.

Discussion also carries with it some epistemological principles which are close to the liberal democratic tradition – principles which place the weight of argument above the weight of authority; principles which stress the importance of exposure to contradiction and criticism as a means of separating sustainable from unsustainable argument and opinion; principles which value the social processes of collaborative construction and deconstruction of meaning, explanation and belief. The procedures which are so central to successful discussion are precisely those which are the heart of an open and democratic society – which provides two more good reasons for placing them centrally in the educational practice of such societies.

Further Readings_____

Bridges, D. (1978) *Education, Democracy, and Discussion*. Windsor, U.K.: NFER Publishing. (Subsequently reissued (1988) by University Press of America).

Burbules, N. (1993) *Dialogue in Teaching: Theory and Practice*. New York: Teachers College Press.

Dillon, J. T. (Ed.) (1988) *Questioning and Discussion: A Multidisciplinary Study.* Norwood, N.J.: Ablex.

What is Controversy?

Terence H. McLaughlin

Controversy arises in relation to many if not all aspects of education and schooling. An appropriately critical understanding of education and schooling requires a grasp of the substance of the various and wide ranging controversies which prevail (including, for example, disputes about the aims, values, content, methodology, assessment, institutionalisation and distribution of learning and teaching). A critical understanding of such matters can be achieved, however, without much reflection on the underlying question of how the notion of controversy itself should be conceived: what matters is the substance of the controversy, rather than the nature of controversy itself.

There is a particular reason, however, why educators should directly address the question 'What is Controversy?' This is because it is widely agreed that education and schooling should engage students in teaching and learning which includes the domain of the controversial. Education and schooling, it is argued, should not shirk a consideration by students of sensitive aspects of questions of a political, social, moral and religious kind. Further, whilst the task of 'teaching controversial issues' is seen in some quarters as confined to questions of these kinds, it is also widely acknowledged that controversial issues arise in relation to many other elements of the curriculum of the school (including, for example, literature, history and science).

Confronting the question 'What is Controversy?' is a necessary, though clearly not sufficient, step which educators need to take in developing and articulating defensible and acceptable principles and strategies for teaching and learning in relation to controversial matters in the face of concerns about pedagogic vices such as bias and indoctrination. For example, in the absence of a clear account of how 'controversy' should be properly understood, neither the conceptualisation and identification of such pedagogic vices nor the conceptualisation and identification of their corresponding pedagogic virtues such as balance and the promotion of critically autonomous judgment can be achieved.

One response to the question 'What is Controversy' is to refer the enquirer to a dictionary. Whilst a dictionary may be a good starting point in achieving clarity, deeper philosophical reflection is needed on the nature of controversy if educationally significant issues are to be brought into clearer focus.

Dictionary definitions of 'controversy' typically identify three general elements in relation to the notion: (i) 'argument,' 'debate,'   (ii) 'disagreement,' 'dispute,' 'contention,' 'contradiction,' 'opposition;' and (iii) 'prolonged,' 'involving many people,' 'arousing strong views,' 'on a matter of opinion which is open to serious disagreement.'

Since not all arguments and debates involve continuing controversy (they could end in agreement) attention can be usefully focused in achieving a clearer understanding of controversy beyond (i) to (ii) and (iii). Whilst 'disagreement', 'dispute' and the like in (ii) are central to the notion of controversy, we need to move beyond (ii) to (iii) to capture the notion of *significant* controversies. Since educators are interested in significant and not merely trivial controversies, (iii) repays careful attention by educators.

Some interpretations of the significance of controversy in (iii) point to social facts such as the duration of the dispute ('prolonged') and its extent ('involving many people'). Other interpretations point to psychological correlates of controversy ('arousing strong views'). Of particular interest educationally are interpretations which point to the *grounding* of the dispute ('on a matter of opinion which is open to serious disagreement'). The most significant disagreements are those which are rooted not merely in contingent social or psychological facts but in deep seated epistemological and ethical considerations which justify us in concluding that the controversy in question is in some sense a reasonable one on which equally rational and well intentioned people may rationally disagree.

The epistemological grounds on which such 'reasonable disagreement' might be based include (a) where insufficient evidence is as yet available to settle a matter, but where such evidence could in principle be forthcoming at some point; (b) where the range of criteria relevant for judging a matter are agreed, but the relative weight to be given to different criteria in a given decision is disputed; (c) where a range of cherished goods cannot simultaneously be realised, and where there is a lack of a clear answer about the grounds on which priorities can be set and adjustments made; (d) where there is no agreement about whole frameworks of understanding relevant for judgment.

The ethical grounds on which 'reasonable disagreement' might be based include considerations relating to a familiar range of first-order moral problems, conflicts and dilemmas which make it necessary to recognise the necessity of moral *judgment* and the possibility of well grounded moral dispute among equally rational and well intentioned people. Such considerations apply also to theoretical and meta-ethical disputes about the nature of the moral and ethical domains and about how matters of (say) conceptualisation and justification in these domains should be approached.

Attention to the nature of controversy, and in particular to the nature of epistemologically and ethically grounded controversy, should furnish educators with important ingredients in developing and articulating defensible and acceptable principles and strategies for teaching and learning in relation to controversial matters.

Teaching and learning in relation to controversial matters involve many issues which go far beyond an answer to the question 'What is Controversy?'. Among complex issues which remain for attention is the identification and selection of particular controversial issues by teachers and schools for consideration by students. In this matter, considerations relating *inter alia* to the nature of the students, parents, the school and its cultural environment require attention: abstract epistemological and ethical considerations alone cannot settle such questions of selection. Such questions are also made more complex by realisation of the point that what actually *is* a controversial issue is itself controversial.

An answer to the question 'What is Controversy' leaves many questions for further attention by educators concerned with teaching and learning in relation to controversial issues. Whilst an answer to the question is clearly insufficient for educators concerned with the domain of the controversial, it is equally clearly necessary.

Further Readings_____

Bridges, D. (1986) Dealing with Controversy in the Curriculum: A Philosophical Perspective, in J. J. Wellington (Ed.), *Controversial Issues in the Curriculum.* Oxford: Blackwell.

Dearden, R. F. (1984) Controversial Issues in the Curriculum, in R. F. Dearden, *Theory and Practice in Education.* London: Routledge and Kegan Paul.

McLaughlin, T. H. (2003) Teaching Controversial Issues in Citizenship Education, in A. Lockyer, B. Crick and J. Annette (Eds.), *Education for Democratic Citizenship: Issues of Theory and Practice.* Aldershot: Ashgate.

What Is Freedom of Speech in Teaching?

Harvey Siegel

What are teachers free to say to their students? Are there limits on teachers' freedom of speech in the classroom? Let us consider cases.

1. *Are teachers free to say things that challenge the beliefs of students or their parents?*

   In many cases, yes. To take an important contemporary example, teachers are free to tell their students that "creation science" does not meet minimal standards of scientific adequacy, and so does not qualify as a *scientific* alternative to evolutionary theory. They are free to do so because it is *true*, according to the criteria of scientific legitimacy governing contemporary scientific theory and practice, that "creation science" does not so qualify. Much has been written about the creationism/evolution controversy; this is not the place to defend the claim just made. Still, the example suggests a general principle concerning teachers' freedom of speech: *(A) Teachers are free to say that which is true.*

Is this principle correct? Though tempting, it needs to be both interpreted and qualified.

1a) A claim's status *as* true – its *truth value* – is often controversial, and so it is risky to rely upon it in determining what teachers are free to say. Even if truth were sufficient to ensure a teacher's freedom to utter that truth, it may be too strong. A more suitable principle may involve, not truth, but rather *rational justification: (B) Teachers are free to say that which they are rationally justified in believing* (i.e., believing to be true).

1b) Truth is not *sufficient* to ensure teachers' freedom of speech: to modify Kant's famous example, if an enraged gun-toting stranger bursts into the classroom and shouts to the teacher "Where is Johnny (your student)? I'm going to kill him!", the teacher is *not* free to reply (truly) "He's in the boys' bathroom down the hall; let me show you." Why not? Because truth is not the only relevant consideration here; the teacher's moral obligation to avoid putting Johnny's life at risk is also relevant to what she is free to say. In so far as saying something is performing an action, moral considerations concerning actions apply to acts of speech as a special case. So a second principle seems to be: *(C) Teachers are **not** free to say anything that it is immoral to say.* Of course moral matters are often controversial. Still, if it is immoral to say something, teachers are not free to say it. And that means that truth – or more weakly, rational justification – is not sufficient to guarantee teachers' freedom of speech.

1c) Is truth or rational justification *necessary*, even if not sufficient, for teachers' freedom of speech? Apparently not: teachers often need to tell their students things which are known to be false. For example, we teach high school students Newtonian physics, even though we know that the universe is not Newtonian. In this and many other cases, we teach students what we take to be age-appropriate *approximations* to what we take to be true or justified, even though we know that those approximations are less worthy, epistemically, than what we take to be the true or best justified view. So *(D) Teachers are free, sometimes, to say that which is false/unjustified*. But teachers can't always do this. For example, teachers aren't free to teach their students systematic falsehoods about a given content area, for this would be mis-educative. This suggests that *(E) Teachers' freedom of speech in the classroom is constrained by their obligation to educate their students*. It would be a useful exercise to explore the conditions under which teachers are/are not free to say that which is false or unjustified. Conducting this exercise would require explicit consideration of the nature and aims of education.

2. *Are teachers free to say things that are offensive to their students or their students' parents, either in content or in tone?*
    Let us consider the cases separately.
    2a) (F) Teachers are indeed free to make pronouncements concerning curricular content that their students (and/or their parents) find offensive. For example, teachers are free to teach their students about evolution, even though some students (or their parents) might find such content offensive. Why are teachers free to risk offense? Because they are trying to *educate* their students, and education can often be, and at its best often is, unsettling and challenging to students' preconceived beliefs. Moreover, because education strives to enhance student autonomy, teachers are free to say things that are educative, even though parents might find their content offensive.
    2b) Nevertheless, teachers are *not* free to teach such potentially offensive content in ways that are needlessly disrespectful or demeaning. The tone in which all content is transmitted must be respectful, because teachers (and all other people) are constrained by the fundamental moral obligation to treat their students (and everyone else) with respect as persons. Thus *(G) Teachers are not free to say things that fail to treat their students with respect as persons*.

3. *Are teachers* **obliged** *to say some things to their students? That is, are they* **not free** *to refrain from telling their students some things?*

    While perhaps counter-intuitive, teachers' freedom of speech is constrained by what they are obliged to say: central age-appropriate truths (or approximations thereof) in their content area, basic information and rules concerning students' health and safety, etc. Hence *(H): Teachers are not free to refrain from saying those things to their students that they are obliged to say.*

    Conclusion: Teachers are indeed free to say quite a lot; their freedom to speak is an important part of both their professional role and status, and their professional obligation to address beliefs, claims and opinions in a way that fosters their students' autonomy and critical thinking. But their freedom is constrained by both moral and epistemological considerations, and so is not 'absolute'; moreover their freedom to *not* say things to their students is limited in that they are obliged to say some things to their students.

    I have offered several principles (*A-H* above) that seem to me to be plausible, or at least worth thinking about. I have not defended any of them at length. They are all debatable, and I offer them not as the last word on the matter, but rather as candidate principles governing teachers' freedom of speech that might be worth further consideration, development, and critical examination. You, dear reader, are free to say what you will in support and/or criticism of them, and I encourage you to exercise that freedom, and to try to come up with better ones.

Further Readings_____

Hostetler, K. D. (1997) *Ethical Judgment In Teaching*. Boston: Allyn and Bacon.

Siegel, H. (1988) *Educating Reason: Rationality, Critical Thinking, and Education*. New York: Routledge.

Siegel, H. (1997) *Rationality Redeemed? Further Essays on an Educational Ideal*. New York: Routledge.

What Is Science Education?

Michael R. Matthews

Science has been one of the most significant contributors to the development of our culture and our understanding of the world. Most thoughtful educators believe that science education should not just be an education or training *in* science, although of course it must be this, but also an education *about* science. Students educated in science should have an appreciation of scientific methods, their diversity and their limitations. Students should have a feeling for methodological issues, such as how scientific theories are evaluated, how experiments are conducted, how evidence bears upon hypothesis appraisal, and how competing theories are appraised. Students doing and interpreting experiments need to know something of how data relies upon theory, how evidence relates to the support or falsification of hypotheses, how real cases relate to ideal cases in science, and a host of other matters which all involve philosophical or methodological concerns. Often this is called an understanding and competence in scientific inquiry.

Teachers of any subject should be able to convey to students something of the intellectual structure of the subject, something of the philosophy of the subject. Students can be engaged by trying to identify the axioms or presuppositions of science: is the law of causality an axiom? Is naturalism an axiom or does science allow 'unnatural' causation? Does science recognise a primary/secondary quality distinction? Or put another way, is nature coloured, does it have aromas, does it have melodious sounds or are these merely features imposed on nature by human sensory capacities? If administrators, teachers and students are told that "evolution is merely a theory" then everyone should be interested in delineating just what a theory is, and how it differs from a law or from a factual claim. Is the hypothetico-deductive method characteristic of science? If it is, then the testing of scientific theories seems to commit the Fallacy of Affirming the Consequent. Good teachers can elaborate on this problem. All of these things require some exposure to and competence in the philosophy of science.

A common occurrence in science classrooms is a child asking: "If no one has seen atoms, how come we are drawing pictures of them?" Such a child is raising one of the most interesting questions in philosophy of science: the relationship of evidence to models, and of models to reality. Good science teachers should encourage such questions and be able to provide satisfactory answers, or suggestions for further questions. To reply "I do not know," or "because it is in the book" is to forego the opportunity of introducing students to the rich methodological dimensions of science.

Students should have some knowledge of the great episodes in the development of science and consequently of culture: the ancient demythologizing of the world picture; the Copernican relocation of the earth from the centre of the solar system; the development of experimental and mathematical science associated with Galileo and Newton; Newton's demonstration that the terrestrial laws of attraction operated in the celestial realms; Darwin's epochal theory of evolution and his claims for a naturalistic understanding of life; Pasteur's discovery of the microbial basis of infection; Einstein's theories of gravitation and relativity; the discovery of the DNA code, and research on the genetic basis of life. They should have an appreciation of the intellectual, technical, social and personal factors that contributed to these monumental achievements.

Although the foregoing expansive view of science education is most often associated with the Liberal Education tradition, a good technical science education also requires some integration of history and philosophy into the program. Knowledge *of* science entails knowledge of scientific facts, laws, theories – the *products* of science; it also entails knowledge of the *processes* of science the technical and intellectual ways in which science develops and tests its knowledge claims. The history and philosophy of science is important for the understanding of these process skills. Students' scientific ability is enhanced if they have read examples of sustained inquiry, clever experimentation, and insightful hypotheses.

To teach Boyle's Law without reflection on what 'law' means in science, without considering what constitutes evidence for a law in science, and without attention to who Boyle was, when he lived, and what he did, is to teach in a truncated way. More can be made of the educational moment than merely teaching, or assisting students to discover that for a given gas at a constant temperature, pressure times volume is a constant, or $PV = k$. Similarly, to teach evolution without considerations concerning theory and evidence, and Darwin's life, times and the religious, literary and philosophical controversies his theory occasioned, is also limited. Likewise the teaching of quantum theory is limited without some inclusion of the life of Planck and his fraught relationship with the Nazi regime; or its teaching without attention to the myriad philosophical issues raised by the theory.

If students are asked to do a simple web search on "Robert Boyle" and "Charles Darwin" countless interesting essays and original texts will be brought up. Students wanting to specialise in science will be enriched by reading some of this material, students destined for other careers will have their understanding of the scientific tradition enriched. Teachers can frame engaging and appropriate project and essay questions that the web pages can be used to answer. Such activities should be part of the expected content of any decent science course.

The account of science education given here is shared by many, including the American Association for the Advancement of Science who in their 1989 landmark *Science for All Americans* wrote that:

> Science courses should place science in its historical perspective. Liberally educated students the science major and the non-major alike should complete their science courses with an appreciation of science as part of an intellectual, social, and cultural tradition. . . . Science courses must convey these aspects of science by stressing its ethical, social, economic, and political dimensions.

Further Readings_____

Matthews, M. R. (Ed.) (1991) *History, Philosophy and Science Teaching: Selected Readings*. Toronto: OISE Press.

Matthews, M. R. (1994) *Science Teaching: The Role of History and Philosophy of Science*. New York: Routledge.

Matthews, M. R. (2000) *Time for Science Education*. New York: Kluwer.

What Is Media Literacy?
Megan Boler

Media education can be defined as the general process of engaging students in "reading the world" of popular culture, news media, and other publicly circulated images and texts. Media literacy is the ability to use the skills of reading visual and media culture. In its most narrow conception, media literacy could be defined as the ability to comprehend the content of a TV program, or to operate a camera. In its best sense, as advocated especially through media education scholarship in the UK, Canada, and Australia, media literacy is recognized as the ability to analyze production, language, audience, and representation within the economic, social, and historical context in which images are produced and read. Just as literacy is not merely about reading but also about writing, so ideally media literacy involves active production of media texts. Perhaps most importantly, media literacy is best thought of as not merely being able to identify and/or use a language or discourse related to film and image, for example, but being able to analyze the social significance of image and media. Specifically, this would mean engaging students in learning to ask: Who produced this? For what audience? To analyze the implication of representation, one would ask: How do we understand a particular image (say, of the contested use of 'multicultural' faces used to sell "United Colors of Benetton") within the larger framework of cultural values and symbols that define the dominant culture? What might be the 'preferred' dominant cultural meaning? Do we necessarily read it that way? How can we understand audiences as always negotiating and often providing 'oppositional' readings of such images?

Media literacy can be well understood by thinking about the two terms. 'Media' refers to the symbol systems, written, print, and visual which are used to communicate in a variety of genres ranging from film, TV, radio, internet, news, popular culture. 'Literacy' is the more difficult to define, since there is a vast and diverse range of conceptions and definitions of literacy. Functional literacy in the most narrow sense is understood to mean the ability to cognitively comprehend and communicate. Paolo Freire revolutionized how we think about literacy, and expanded literacy to mean not simply abilities to read and write but to "read the world." Freire's vision encompasses a recognition that, first, what we read is always situated in a culture and history of power; and second, that in developing a praxis of reading the world, we gain access to a world of power by honing the critical ability to redefine terms and thereby re-evaluate our relationship to the dominant culture.

Because we increasingly live in cultures saturated with media, and because media exerts tremendous influence in the shaping of our cultural and personal identities, the ability to 'critically' analyze media opens doors to discourse and power. While the word 'critical' is contested and often used too broadly, "critical media literacy" can be understood as situating analyses of media within their economic, historical, and political context. So for example, one might engage students in analysis of advertising and its influence; research into the corporate influence in mainstream news, TV, and film; and develop skills of production to encourage participation as active citizens of the media world.

Media literacy is often defined with a sense of social and political agency in mind. In Canada, the Association of Media Literacy (AML) has pioneered work in the area of media literacy, and Canadian media educator Barry Duncan makes an important distinction between "teaching about media" and "teaching through media." Teaching through media would be having students watch a documentary or film with no critical reflection about the form, perspective, context, and so on, of the media text. "Teaching about media" would include pointed discussion and active development of skills that engage questions about the construction of the form of the media itself: Whose point of view is used to tell the story? What camera angles are used and how does this shape the audience positioning in relation to the narrative? Who is the intended audience and how does this shape the narrative and message? Who funded the project and has this shaped the content?

There is increasing emphasis on production as part of media education. While early schools of thought tended to push for media literacy as a means to critique dominant ideologies, one finds increasing arguments for pleasure as part of media education – whether pleasure in production and reception, or the pleasure of video games and a recognition that gaming culture is an advanced form of multimodal literacy that involves collaboration and community.

Perhaps the most polarized debate within educational discourses about media can be characterized as protectionism vs. critical engagement. The 'protectionist' discourse situates students as innocent children requiring others to judge the value and merit of what the student should or should not be permitted to view/play/engage with. This view would 'protect' students from the perceived 'evils' of media, whether evil is defined as Disney films, or the negative effects of advertising, or exposure to particular ideological messages. The protectionist discourse understands media in terms of a causal model: for example, it would argue that watching violence necessarily leads to increased violent behavior or adoption of beliefs or values seen as less than desirable. In contrast to the protectionist model, those who advocate critical engagement would prefer to see education create spaces for public discussion about popular culture rather than simply policing and penalizing. The latter view – that we need greater public spaces in education to engage media literacy – speaks clearly to the need (a) for curricula standards to recognize media as a legitimate subject area; (b) for teacher education programs to prepare K-12 teachers to teach "about media;" (c) for schools to recognize the radically changing modes of literacy within contemporary digital and technological culture.

Examples of the intersection of media literacy and production include practices such as culture jamming and digital storytelling. Culture jamming refers to a long history of subcultural practices concerned with countering dominant or fascist ideologies through diverse forms ranging from creative rearrangement of billboards, to counter-broadcasts or broadcast interruptions, to hactivism, to underground publishing. Digital storytelling refers to multimedia compositions of original work, often supported through a university-school or university-community partnership, that gives young people (often in urban areas) an opportunity to work with new media and combine texts, spoken word, song, and still and moving images, to create stories about cultural experience and identities.

Further Readings_____
Buckingham, D. (2003) *Media Education: Literacy, Learning and Contemporary Culture.*
    Cambridge: Polity Press.
Duncan, B., et al. (1996) *Mass Media and Popular Culture.* Toronto: Harcourt Brace.
Media Literacy Online Project. **http://interact.uoregon.edu/MediaLit/HomePage**

What Is Student Engagement?

John P. Portelli

Student engagement has been described as an elusive and contested concept since its meaning is not always clear and differing competing meanings and definitions have been associated with the term. Nonetheless there is a "family of concepts" that can be readily associated with the term and another that is usually contrasted with student engagement. For example, while terms such as "connections, connectedness, relations, commitment, promise, closeness, belonging, involvement, inspired, interested, motivated, attachment, integration, concentration and effort, ownership, empowerment, authenticity and responsibility" remind us of some aspect of engagement, terms such as "alienation, isolation, separation, detachment, fragmentation, and boredom" are associated with a lack of engagement or even disengagement.

Some have even used metaphors to clarify the concept of engagement. Two common metaphors are the "gear metaphor" and the "engagement as promise of marriage metaphor." The former one highlights the *quality* of the engagement and replaces images of students following routines, blindly completing assignments, or maximizing "time on task." Just like an engaged clutch of an engine, student engagement should involve a harnessing of energy and a meaningful movement forward. The latter metaphor highlights the elements of trust, responsibility, commitment and future orientation. The complexity of student engagement increases when one notes that it is not always necessarily observable (that is it could be personal or private), it involves a certain kind of relationship with peers, texts, educators, and community members that implies some hope, commitment, and possibilities, and it is contingent or context dependent. Student engagement is co-constructed and developed over a period of time.

Since the 1990s "student engagement" has become a popular catch phrase and subject of empirical research in education. Consequently, one may be left with the impression that it is a new phenomenon. However, a cursory glance at the development of educational theory in the western world, shows that the connection between engagement and educative learning has a long tradition. For example, the perennial question of the justification of a worthwhile curriculum dates to the work of Plato and Aristotle and reappears in other periods as exemplified in Herbert Spencer's question, "What knowledge is of most worth?" Augustine discusses the importance of the student in the learning process. Rousseau, Montessori, and Dewey emphasize the importance of the individual and social needs of the student. And Freire and other critical and feminist pedagogues argue for the necessity of praxis and democratic practices. These issues involve and are directly linked to the connection between engagement and learning.

Why is it important to focus on student engagement? Given that no one reasonably desires disengagement or lack of engagement, one could argue that its importance is self-evident. Student engagement is indisputably a worthwhile educational aim. Education, in its very nature, is inconsistent with the promotion of an alienated learner, in the same way as it is incompatible with indoctrination. The elusiveness of the concept and the need for further clarification offers another justification for focusing on student engagement. Not all learners that seem to be engaged from the perspective of the teacher are necessarily engaged, and not all learners that seem to be disengaged are necessarily disengaged. Since substantively different conceptions of engagement have emerged, we need to examine the different practical implications that arise from them as well as the underlying epistemological and educational beliefs. And since some of these implications and beliefs are not consistent with each other, we are then faced with the following moral or ethical questions: Which conception of engagement is more worthwhile or suitable? Are all forms of student engagement equally valuable? Whose conception of engagement is considered to be most worthwhile? The latter question inevitably leads us into the realm of issues of power and ideology, and hence the raising of the broader question: What are the specific purposes of student engagement and who benefits or gets marginalized, and possibly even excluded, from these purposes?

Mainstream research on student engagement has been of an empirical nature, more specifically of a technical and/or psychological bent. Most of this work focuses on attempts to identify the different forms student engagement takes in school, or on the conditions, practices, strategies, skills and policies that either enhance or hinder student engagement. This work has resulted in some informative data. For example, that meaningful student engagement is enhanced by helping students construct positive self-images, ensuring positive and appropriate constructions of students by educators, exhibiting willingness on the part of teachers to communicate humanely and fairly with students and caring about students as persons, and developing democratic communities in schools. Conversely, having low academic expectations of students, adopting a deficit mentality toward students, and turning schools into bureaucratic institutions contribute to student disengagement.

Unfortunately, most of these studies have lacked a certain philosophical rigour and have failed to inquire into the very foundations of the conceptions of student engagement that arise from the popular discourse and that in fact guides this work. The majority of prescriptive or stipulative definitions offered explicitly or implicitly promote a conception of engagement conceived of as a neutral or technical process. In these cases, the role of researcher is to 'objectively' identify the conditions of learning that can be altered or controlled to promote student engagement. However, such a perspective begs the foundational questions of the meaning and purposes of engagement, and fails to consider the complexities and the moral and political aspects of engagement while at the same time promoting a linear or simple cause-effect characterization of engagement.

A more meaningful and critical perspective of student engagement needs to take into account questions such as: What and whose purposes of education and constructions of educational success determine student engagement? How might student engagement be reconceived to include the goals of equity, social justice and academic excellence? How does the pathologizing of non-mainstream students hinder us from a better understanding of disengagement? It has been suggested that such a conception of engagement would have to go beyond a reductionist or technical perspective to include a way of being guided by the democratic values of equity, social justice, and inclusion and one that guides teaching, curriculum, leadership and policy.

Further Readings_____
Butler-Kisber, L. and Portelli, J. P. (Eds.) (2003) *McGill Journal of Education* 38, (2). Special issue on Student Engagement.
McMahon, B. & Portelli, J.P. (2004) Engagement for What? Beyond Popular Discourses of Student Engagement, *Leadership and Policy in Schools* 3, (1): 59-76.
Newmann, F. (Ed.) (1992) *Student Engagement and Achievement in American Schools.* New York: Teachers College Press.

What Is A Good School?
Carolyn M. Shields

Socrates is often credited with the statement that "the unexamined life is not worth living." Building on this statement, a good school is one that teaches students how to lead an examined life. It may be recognized by the extent to which it facilitates disciplined inquiry, careful reflection, social justice, and new understandings about topics that matter.

A good school is an inclusive community – not one that is homogeneous and expects people to "fit in", but one that is created from the diverse contributions and abilities of its members. People are not excluded based on the colour of their skin, their socio-economic status, or their cultural affiliation. There is no deficit thinking, no assumptions that some are more worthy of respect than others based on such things as linguistic ability, prior experience, or group affiliation. In a good school, all members of the school community learn from one another.

A good school promotes the development of students who are able to ask as well as answer questions and to reflect and critique rather than to simply receive information. It helps students to develop openness to others, to doubt and to inquire rather than simply to take an unquestioned position and argue it with arrogant certainty. It raises questions about equity as well as excellence and helps students develop criteria to make decisions about alternative perspectives. A good school teaches students to consider both individual benefit and the collective good.

The foundation of the school community is strong interpersonal relationships and ongoing dialogue. The good school community is a place in which the goal is to treat each other with singular regard, in which each person is known, supported, and valued. Members of the community contribute differently, yet meaningfully, through their unique talents, interests, and perspectives. A good school is a place (both literal and figurative) in which the dynamic inquiry helps people to understand how to live together in just and caring relationships. It is a place in which the inquiry is fervent, marked by fierce debate, persuasive arguments, and pointed questions, for such are the tools of learning and understanding. Each person's voice is valued; each person's perspective is heard and considered respectfully. The goal is not unquestioned acceptance of a particular perspective, but carefully examined concepts about what is worthwhile and meaningful. A good school is one in which all members of the community accept diversity, embrace ambiguity, welcome creative conflict, and learn from one another. This focus on community, relationships, and dialogue has implications for pedagogy, curriculum, assessment, and leadership.

Pedagogy in a good school is not one of transmission, but one of relations. It requires meeting one another in what Buber calls an I-Thou relationship. In a good school, teaching is not defined as the ability to impart information to students, but the ability to facilitate inquiry and help students develop understanding about new ideas. Pedagogy is understood as the creation of spaces in which all learners may bring the totality of their lived experience – their spirituality, ethnicity, culture, socio-economic conditions, political ideologies, and practical experiences – as a basis for engaging in the sense-making conversations that are the fabric of the school.

In a good school students learn more than they are taught. They construct, embellish, explore, challenge – bringing life and meaning to the various ideas that are presented. Educators recognize that curriculum is dynamic. The curriculum is not simply the formal learning objectives identified by the overseeing jurisdiction, not the disconnected items of information presented in texts, but the inquiry, the examination of what makes life worthwhile. It grows from the community's dialogue itself. The curriculum comes to life when learners understand that information and knowledge are not synonyms. Instead, information must be socially constructed, situated, and understood to become knowledge. Curriculum as conversation becomes the basis for children and adults together to learn to challenge those aspects of our society that preclude a worthwhile life for some members of society, to overcome inequity, and to understand and root out prejudice of all kinds – individual, institutional, and systemic. The prescribed curriculum is never an end in itself, but the basis for the impassioned dialogue.

It follows, therefore, that assessment in a good school is the monitoring of the conversations about what is worthwhile and what is not, the identification of questions still unanswered as well as responses given and reflected upon. It includes, but is never limited to, the basic accomplishment of objectives appropriate to a student's age and grade. Some of these objectives may be easily assessed (decoding, computation, and so forth); others (such as civics, global citizenship) are more nebulous, but no less important. Despite current strategies that emphasize accountability and attempt to determine the worth or 'goodness' of a school based on relatively narrow test-based measures of student achievement, the worth of a good school is found in the quality of life it promotes for all members of its community.

Leadership in a good school is fluid. It is never simply positional, although those in formally identified roles must be both leaders and good managers. Strong leadership requires the moral use of power, the ability to make just decisions, to intervene with integrity and purpose to promote a worthwhile life for all members of the community. Educators deliberately intervene in the lives of students, mandating their attendance at school, engaging them in learning, and assessing their progress in order to open windows of understanding and doors of opportunity to each one.

If a worthwhile life is an examined one, then a good school is the learning community that sets students on the path of inquiry and gives them the tools of reflection, dialogue, and critique to be successful. Although it may sound naïve and optimistic to those jaded by present educational debates about accountability and ideology, a good school is transformative. It is an instrument of meaningful change in the lives of individual students, their families, and the wider society.

Further Readings_____
Palmer, P. J. (1998) *The Courage to Teach: Exploring the Inner Landscape of a Teacher's Life*. San Francisco: Jossey-Bass.
Shields, C. M. (2003) *Good Intentions Are Not Enough: Transformative Leadership for a Community of Difference*. Lanham, M.D.: Scarecrow.
Sidorkin, A. M. (1999) *Beyond Discourse: Education, the Self, and Dialogue*. New York: State University of New York Press.

 # What Is Progressive Education?

Michael J. B. Jackson • Douglas J. Simpson

CENTRAL FIGURES AND IDEAS

The diverse intellectual roots of progressive education in the West, but also worldwide, usually include Jean-Jacques Rousseau (1712-1778), Johann Heinrich Pestalozzi (1746-1827), Johann Friedrich Herbart (1776-1841), Friedrich Froebel (1782-1852), Maria Montessori (1870-1952), and John Dewey (1859-1952). Their ideas were both applied and misapplied to schools and classroom practices, leading to local and national trends sometimes described as a 'movement'. Central ideas, although varied and nuanced, typically include (1) the value of early childhood education, (2) the importance of the whole child, (3) the use of first-hand experience in learning, (4) the relevance of the child's world for teaching, (5) the school's need to adapt its pedagogy to the student, (6) the child's understanding as the starting point of curricular choices, (7) democratic ideals in selecting classroom activities, and (8) understanding children. Progressive education opposed practices focused largely or exclusively on lecturing to students, imparting pre-packaged information, securing learning by drill and memorization, and using externally enforced discipline and evaluation to control learning and behaviour.

The most fundamental questions in education include: What should we *teach*, to whom, when, how, and why? A progressive educator might rather ask: What should a child *learn*, when, how, and why? Popularly, traditional education is associated with instruction in the academic disciplines; progressive education with guided learning activities, often in groups, using children's immediate interests and settings and intended to enrich their everyday lives. Traditional education stresses teaching, progressive education stresses learning; but both, at their best, emphasize each child's achieving genuine knowledge and understanding. Disagreements centre on how best to do so, notably the stress placed on children's activities and everyday experiences, and how understanding and knowledge are achieved.

FUNDAMENTAL QUESTIONS

Some see education as preparation for living in the present in anticipation of a heavenly realm or its secular equivalent; others as pursuing academic or personal excellence; still others as preparing people for roles in society, productive jobs, and enjoyable lives. Contemporary education increasingly emphasizes enabling everyone to understand the world and to participate in the direction of their lives and communities. The aims of progressive education resemble this modern set and, at their best, are associated with genuine understanding, power, and democratic citizenship. Progressive practices, therefore, promote personal understanding, self-direction, and democratic involvement.

Proponents and opponents criticize certain strands of progressive education for neglecting academic subjects, especially the sciences, languages, and literature. Dewey, for example, to distance his views from some other views of progressive education, emphasized the value of past and present knowledge and reflective thinking in developing critical, informed minds and active, democratic citizens: he wanted to distinguish what he considered education from training and socialization. Thus, he and traditionalists differed less about what knowledge and abilities are of most educational worth than about several largely empirical questions of which means work, when and for whom, and whether certain means are likely or even able to promote or show genuine understanding. Despite extreme stereotypes, informed thoughtful disagreements that merit evaluation typically are not about whether the traditional disciplines are worthwhile or should be learned, but whether they can be properly learned and assessed other than by direct instruction and formal examinations and whether schooling should be separated from the student's growth at home and in the community.

That both traditional teachers, using high expectations and direct instruction, and progressive teachers succeed suggests that, beyond the progressive-traditional dichotomy, a teacher's style of teaching is important and that we should not expect or require all teachers to teach the same way. Each approach is successful and often desirable, particularly for some children; neither is always necessary. So, a progressive approach should allow teachers the freedom to develop unique styles, provided the means and ends are ethical, effective, and efficient.

CONCLUSIONS

What was – and is – 'progressive' about progressive education? It emphasized *new* child-centred approaches and thinking. But it is not a single, unified movement, and competing claims, arguments, and uses of the term remain, emerge, and may deserve attention. We hold that its basic principle is shared by all who believe that more children can learn, learn more, and learn better if how they are taught is better adapted to them and their worlds. In this sense, nearly all teachers are progressive, and the debate about being progressive is now a false one: who would want to be regressive or unprogressive? We all want children to learn as much of what is worth knowing – better, *understanding* – as they can: that is the only legitimate reason for teaching, the aim of which is to promote learning, usually learning what is worth learning.

We may differ about what progress is; but, if understanding and informed, thoughtful action are our goal, debate about progressive education is typically about the merits of a particular curriculum or examination: about how much of, how soon, and how directly the standard disciplines should appear, and which teaching, learning, and evaluation strategies work best and for which children and when. What is controversial is *the extent to which the child's immediate experience is helpful in promoting and assessing learning* and how success should be measured. These are largely empirical questions, though they also hinge on our conceptions of success, an educated person, and progress.

The real opponents of progressive education, then, include those who favour life adjustment or training people for certain roles in society, have a limited view of what people can or should learn and understand, wish to indoctrinate students into a particular way of living and thinking, and wish to determine the role of students in society and in social and political decision-making.

Further Readings_____

Collins, III, J. W., & O'Brien, N. P. (2003) Progressive Education, in *The Greenwood Dictionary of Education*. Westport, C.T.: Greenwood Press.

Dejnozka, E. L., & Kapel, D. E. (1982) Progressive Education, in *American Educators' Encyclopedia*. Westport, C.T.: Greenwood Press.

Dewey, J. (1997) *Experience and Education*. New York: Touchstone.

What Is Democratic Education?

Ronald David Glass

I want to explore the question "What is Democratic Education?" by sketching some of the principles that would enable education (and more specifically, public schooling) to foster the development of critical, engaged citizens committed both to creating a robust participatory and pluralistic democracy and to pursuing justice.

Today, what kind of citizen is developed through schooling? For the most part, public schools integrate the generations into the logics of the dominant ideologies through the coercive ranking and sorting regimes that permeate their social and academic practices. Students' identities are conformed to norms and standards that favour the status quo and make them more or less like anybody else of their race, class, gender, or abilities. Anybody in school learns to blame only her/himself if s/he does not meet the school's expectations, and to accept with pride of personal achievement the privileges that come with measuring up. Anybody in school learns to accept school academic performances as the measure of her/his social, economic, and political worth and opportunities beyond school. Those who cannot or will not conform are marginalized into nobodies, people not expected to contribute to the school and community, to be intelligent or know much of value, or to be articulate or say much that anybody wants to hear. Nobodies are told to look to their own moral and intellectual shortcomings as the causes of their failure because every nobody supposedly had the same opportunity as anybody else to be successful and become somebody. Those who are somebody in school are of two types, either exceptionally good (the best of the anybodies) or exceptionally bad (the baddest of the nobodies). But these somebodies leave the school's dominant norms and standards intact, reinscribing the unjust social order. In other words, the social and academic practices of public schools mostly develop forms of identity that undercut the kind of self-understanding required for critical democratic citizenship.

The kind of citizenship that should be the aim of a democratic education requires a different kind of somebody to be formed through the process of schooling, a somebody-in-particular who understands that identity formation in schools occurs within politically charged historical, social, and cultural horizons. This somebody-in-particular sees behind the common sense dominant norms and standards of the day and achieves a critical grasp of their underlying struggles and debates as well as a critical grasp of the inalienable power each person has to shape those ideological conflicts. Democratic education enables students to develop the capacities needed to challenge the limits of the current situation and transform the world toward a vision of a more just democratic community. Democratic citizenship entails creative effort to build a new reality through that collaborative struggle. Neither democracy nor citizenship can be bestowed or achieved by proclamation; both necessitate enduring commitments to a way of life that instantiates principles of fairness and participation so that each and every person is a valued member of the community. A democratic education worthy of the name refuses to make a nobody of anybody.

We live in a pluralistic, diverse society in which many varieties of custom, mores, culture, religion and practical reason condition morality and politics, and thus conflicts are endemic to moral and political matters no less than to economic and social life. A diversity of ideals of the person and of the best social and political arrangements for democracy to flourish is inescapable. Thus a democratic public education has a special responsibility to prepare citizens to engage with these conflicts as a central duty of democratic life itself. In order for these conflicts to extend the scope and application of morality and justice and to enrich the democracy, they must occur within the constraints of agreements about deliberative processes and about the limits of more coercive forms of disagreement. Since political conflicts will be resolved either by argument or force, citizens should be skilled in the arts of deliberation if tyranny is not to rule. Beyond this, however, because rationality is a weak bond and likely to fail at crucial points, citizens need additional principles and methods of action that command their loyalty and secure civil society despite multiple conceptions of the right and good. These are principles of militant nonviolence, which balance persuasive and coercive powers in powerful forms of political action (such as civil disobedience) that avoid might making right or domination by force.

Citizens schooled in the necessary skills of critique of the dominant ideologies, of understanding diverse views, of engaging in complex negotiations, and of collective nonviolent action can embody democratic processes that over time facilitate the clash of competing ideas and policies so that more evils and injustices become regarded not as givens but rather as moral and political failures subject to melioration. In pluralistic democratic societies, such matters occupy the major portion of public debate and of the business of political and social institutions, and are the major preoccupations of citizen activism. Pluralist critical democratic citizens have no way to resolve disputes outside the ways created through those very processes of deliberation and struggle.

Democratic citizenship is hard work. If citizenship is merely about what we are entitled to from the state and what minimal loyalties and obligations we owe in return, then democracy is imperiled. If we cannot authentically participate in the direction of society, we cannot be full citizens. Democratic citizenship must be understood as the actual creation of civil society and the state, and as the concomitant struggle for justice that provides the possibility of equal citizenship, of genuinely equal rights, opportunities, and capacities to govern or rule. Democratic deliberative processes recognize the moral agency of participants, seek agreement through shared reasons and reflection in public venues, and require mutual accountability. Democratic citizenship is morally demanding and requires a robust participation in the formation of society. This sort of active citizenship operates most meaningfully at the level of the community where our most heartfelt plural identities get enacted through organizations and institutions (churches, synagogues, mosques, unions, parties, civic and service groups, etc.). Here, the self-determination of the citizen is not abstract, and citizens engaged in these ways are both more likely to be resistant to ideological manipulation and to demand that their representatives be accountable. This strengthens democracy even though the multiple commitments and loyalties of the citizen also engender or amplify conflicts. Yet the more that citizens participate in the wide range of activities that form a just community, the more these conflicts find voice and then possible resolution within democratic institutions. Critical activist citizens are the antidote to tyranny, the guardians of democracy, and the engines of justice.

Democratic education does not simply prepare students for a future citizenship, but rather builds critical citizenship into the social and academic practices of the school. The dominant ideologies that undermine democracy and perpetuate injustice do not stop at the schoolhouse door and because they permeate in various forms the curriculum, processes, and structures of schooling, democratic education directly struggles to transform the inequities in the immediacy of everyday life in schools. Democratic education facilitates the formation of somebodies-in-particular, citizens who intentionally embody their power to make history and culture in the quest for a just pluralistic democracy.

Further Readings_____

Freire, P. (1993) *Pedagogy of the Oppressed.* (Revised 20th Anniversary Edition). New York: Continuum.

Freire, P. (1999) *Pedagogy of Freedom: Ethics, Democracy, and Civic Courage.* Lanham, M.D.: Rowman & Littlefield.

Gutmann, A. & Thompson, D. (1996) *Democracy and Disagreement.* Cambridge, M.A.: The Belknap Press of Harvard University Press.

What Is Multiculturalism?

Pradeep A. Dhillon

It is important to maintain the various senses of the terms 'multiculturalism' and "multicultural education" in order to obtain a clearer view of what is at stake in their use in educational discourse. The distinctions thus drawn grow in significance when we consider the risks, moral and political, that we run in conflating the two terms. At the very least, multiculturalism signifies the diversity of forms of life which constitute a polity. Multicultural education, on the other hand, is the response of a polity to managing cultural diversity. In other words, historically societies have always contained different groups with differing practices, values, and traditions within them. This was true of social organizations in Greek and Indian antiquity, for example, as it is today. Educational responses to such given diversity, with a view to fostering social and political cohesion while maintaining the dignity of the members of a polity, however, have been various and different – ranging from the reprehensible practices of ethnic cleansing to the utopian view of a free and unfettered pluralism.

'Multiculturalism' also carries the sense of an orientation in thinking. This sense addressed by Thoreau, Nussbaum and Cavell, among others, appeals to moral judgment in refusing to value one set of practices and traditions, usually one's own, over that of others both within a liberal-democratic state such the United States, and globally. It suggests a way of thinking whereby we are open to the value of different forms of life, not in the spirit of tolerance alone, but with a sense of being part of flexible and expanding social and cultural networks. Learning about others, on this view, is learning more deeply about ourselves. It is this sort of thinking which prompts the preservation of world heritage sites around the globe and permits the enjoyment of Kumar Gandharva's *Raag Bhageshwari* with as keen an aesthetic response as one might bring to YoYo Ma's renditions of Bach's

Partitas. Multicultural education would facilitate the achievement of such cosmopolitan pleasures as well as provide us with a more enlightened and enriched way of life. That is, multicultural education would seek to foster both the attitude of 'multiculturalism' – a non-hierarchical view about the distribution of cultures within a nation-state and across the globe – and knowledge about the aesthetic and intellectual traditions of various cultures.

'Multiculturalism' in its political sense has come to mean the insistence on the recognition of the value of other cultures and the significance of such recognition for the sense of well being of all the members of a liberal-democratic state. Argued most cogently by Charles Taylor, on this view, we are not only invited to think about the varieties of culture existing within and across our borders, but also acknowledge that power relations, social and historical as obtained through the institutions of slavery and colonialism, for example, shape our engagement with other cultures and even our own. Such relations have created majority-minority traditions nationally, and globally, with consequences for equal and full social, economic, and legal, participation. It is argued, that since the identities of individuals are formed through interactions with other members of their cultural group, they are denied the basic dignity and opportunities for flourishing promised by the liberal democratic state when the status of their group is diminished. Furthermore, on this view, liberal democratic states are held responsible for the preservation of the cultural integrity necessary for such human flourishing. Political multicultural educational discourse seeks to bring to the fore the historical development of such asymmetries of power. This approach not only seeks to redress historical oversight but also undermines the view that some cultures and their members are 'naturally' inferior to others.

The educational response to this sense of multiculturalism serves another significant purpose and that is the proper dispensation of justice. Jurgen Habermas argues, for example, that such education is necessary if we are to reconcile *de facto* and *de jure* juridical practices. Habermas's approach is particularly attractive for it seeks to reconcile the general philosophical principles of justice as articulated by John Rawls, with the worry about the specific cultural conditions under which such justice is practised, and often *mis*-practised as argued by Jean-Francois Lyotard and Michael Sandel among others. Multicultural education is vital for the effective functioning of a liberal-democratic state where equality before the law cannot be achieved through empty commitments to neutrality but rather only through deep and thorough understanding of the various cultures that form their socio-political fabric. Shakespeare's *Merchant of Venice* is a fine example of the failure of justice when neutrality, unmitigated by multicultural education, is assumed in a multicultural state.

In sum, then, the terms 'multiculturalism' and 'multicultural education' are certainly good descriptors of how our worlds are, and have been. However, they also serve as prescriptions for the full realization of the liberal-democratic ideals that inspire not only most of the Western states, but also much of the rest of the world, as also global institutions, such as the United Nations. Nevertheless, we could ask, are multiculturalism and multicultural education unmitigated goods? Not everyone, including those committed to liberal-democratic values would agree. The two principal objections raised by feminists and individual members of historically devalued cultural groups rest on the criticism that multicultural theorists have often taken cultures to be closed and undifferentiated. Hence, philosophers like Susan Okin and Kwame Anthony Appiah argue the rights of sub-groups, such as those of women and other minorities within a culture, could be over-ridden by multicultural concerns. That is, 'essentialist' readings of a culture may lead us to missing, or even worse, supporting, the continued oppression of say African-American women within the United States, or the *dalits* of India. Furthermore, as pointed out so poignantly by Appiah, recognition of a minority cultural group may cause us to overlook the struggles of individuals and deny them dignity, limit their possibilities for flourishing, and refuse their right to draw and choose their own life trajectories. Such oversight, resulting from too strong a commitment to the rights of minority groups at the cost of individual rights – sacrificing autonomy to authenticity – runs the danger of reinscribing stereotypes, and locking in individual hopes and choices; thus, leaving the power in the hands of well-intentioned members of the dominant group. Finally, a bounded understanding of cultural variation runs the risk of closing off inter-cultural communication vital to the healthy functioning of liberal-democratic societies nationally and at the global level. This philosophical and educational story has a long history, is unfinished, and is being written with increasing sophistication.

Further Readings_____

Benhabib, S. (2002) *The Claims of Culture: Equality and Diversity in the Global Era.*
    Princeton, N.J.: Princeton University Press.
Feinberg, W. (2000) *Common Schools/Uncommon Identities: National Unity and
    Cultural Difference.* New Haven: Yale University Press.
Okin, S. M., Cohen, J., Howard, M., & Nussbaum, M. (Eds.) (1999) *Is
    Multiculturalism Bad for Women?* Princeton, NJ.: Princeton University Press.

What Is Critical Pedagogy?

Antonia Darder

Critical pedagogy is a school of thought that emerged in the twentieth century. Steeped in a long tradition of critical social thought and progressive educational movements, critical pedagogy links the practice of schooling to democratic principles of society and to transformative social action. An underlying and explicit intent of critical pedagogy is a commitment to the unwavering liberation of oppressed populations and a belief in the historical possibility of change. Critical pedagogy represents a significant attempt to bring together divergent radical views of education. Although, there is no recipe for the universal implementation and application of any form of critical pedagogy, its philosophical principles are founded on a critical theoretical tradition. Influential to its theoretical formation are the major theorists of the Frankfurt School, along with Antonio Gramsci, Michel Foucault, and, more recently, Jurgen Habermas. Critical educational theorists drew upon the work of these thinkers to develop their notions of a critical pedagogy. Three of the most influential contemporary educational theorists are Paulo Freire, Henry Giroux and Peter McLaren. The following provides a brief introduction to the principles that underlie a critical pedagogy.

1. **Cultural Politics:** Critical pedagogy is committed to the development of a classroom culture that supports the empowerment of culturally and economically marginalized students. This pedagogical perspective seeks to transform classroom structures and practices that stifle democratic life. A critical analysis of traditional theories and practices of public schooling are considered fundamental to an emancipatory and humanizing culture of participation, voice and social action. Critical pedagogy calls upon teachers to acknowledge how schools are founded on theories and practices that unite knowledge and power, in ways that sustain inequality and exclusion under the guise of neutral and apolitical views of education. Thus, schools function as a cultural terrain where struggles for legitimate knowledge are ongoing.

2. **Political Economy:** Critical pedagogy contends that traditional schooling works against the class interests of those students most politically and economically vulnerable. The competing role of the marketplace in the production of knowledge and in the structural relationships and policies that shape public schools is recognized as a significant factor. Public schools replicate the existing values and privileges of the dominant class, through hierarchical practices such as testing and tracking of students. It is this uncontested relationship between schools and society that critical pedagogy seeks to challenge, unmasking false claims that education provides equal opportunity and access for all. In the process of class reproduction, schooling practices are deceptively organized to perpetuate gendered, racialized and sexual inequalities.

3. **Historicity of Knowledge:** Critical pedagogy contends that all knowledge is created within a historical context that gives life and meaning to human experience. Schools are understood within the boundaries of social practice and the historical events that inform educational policies. Similarly, students and the knowledge they bring into the classroom are understood as historical. That is, schools are constructed and produced within particular historical moments and under particular historical conditions. Critical pedagogy urges teachers to create opportunities in which students understand themselves as

subjects of history and recognize conditions of injustice as historically produced. This historical view of knowledge offers an analysis that stresses the breaks, discontinuities, conflicts, differences, and tensions in history, which highlight the centrality of social agency and the possibilities for change.

4. **Dialectical Theory:** Unlike traditional theories of education that reinforce certainty, conformity, and technical control of knowledge and power, critical pedagogy embraces a dialectical view of knowledge. A dialectical perspective begins, first and foremost, with human existence and the contradictions and disjunctions that both shape and make problematic its meaning. Hence, the problems of society are not seen as mere random or isolated events, but rather as moments that arise out of the interaction between the individual and society. Rooted in a dialectical view of knowledge, critical pedagogy encourages the dynamic interactive elements, rather than the formation of dichotomies and polarizations in thought and practice. A dialectical view stresses the power of human activity and human knowledge as both a product and a force in shaping the world.

5. **Ideology and Critique:** Ideology refers to a framework of thought used to give order and meaning to the social and political world. Ideology generally exists at the deep, embedded structures of the personality. Manifesting itself as 'commonsense' it is rooted in individual needs, drives, and passions, as well as the changing material conditions of society. This critical notion of ideology provides the means for a critique of educational curricula, texts and practices, as well as the interests that inform their production. Pedagogically, ideology is used to unmask the contradictions that exist between the mainstream culture and the lived experiences and knowledge that students use to mediate school life. Hence, ideology is an important starting point for posing questions that will help teachers to evaluate critically their practice. Through such critique, teachers can better recognize how the culture of the dominant class is embedded in the hidden curriculum, informed by ideological views that thwart democratic education.

6. **Hegemony:** Hegemony refers to a process of social control that is carried out through the moral and intellectual leadership of a dominant class over subordinate groups. Critical pedagogy incorporates this notion of hegemony in order to demystify inequalities and the social arrangements that sustain the interest of the ruling class. Hegemony points to the powerful connection that exists between politics, economics, culture, and pedagogy. Teachers are challenged to critique and transform classroom conditions tied to hegemonic processes, which perpetuate the economic and cultural marginalization of subordinate groups. This process of critique is understood as an ongoing process, for hegemony is neither static nor absolute. Understanding how hegemony functions in society provides educators with the basis for comprehending how domination is reproduced and how inequalities can be challenged and overcome, through resistance, critique and social action.

7. **Resistance and Counter Hegemony:** A theory of resistance begins with the assumption that all people have the capacity to produce knowledge and resist domination. However, how they choose to resist is clearly influenced and limited by the social and material conditions that shape their lives and the ideological formations internalized in the process. Counter-hegemony refers to those intellectual and social spaces where power relationships are reconstructed to make central the voices and experiences of those existing in the margins of society. Counter-hegemonic contexts are forged out of moments of resistance, through establishing alternative structures and practices that democratize relations of power, in the interest of liberatory possibilities.

8. **Praxis**: The idea that theory and practice are inextricably linked is key to critical pedagogy. Hence, all theory is considered with respect to its practical intent. Unlike schooling practices that emphasize instrumental/technical application of theory, critical practices are conceived as self-creating and self-generating free human activity. Human activity is understood as emerging from the ongoing interaction of reflection, dialogue and action – namely praxis. Theory, in alliance with practice, illuminates the world, both as we find it and as it might

be. This alliance of theory and practice opens the way for concrete social change.

9. **Dialogue and Conscientization:** Dialogue speaks to an emancipatory educational process that is, above all, committed to the empowerment of students. Critical dialogue challenges the dominant educational discourse, illuminating the right and freedom of students to become subjects of their world. Dialogue as an emancipatory educational strategy centers upon the development of critical social consciousness or what Freire termed '*conscientizaçao.*' Conscientization is the process by which students, as empowered subjects, achieve a deepening awareness of the social realities that shape their lives and discover their own capacities to recreate them.

Further Readings_____

Darder, A, Baltodano, M. & Torres R. D. (2002) *Critical Pedagogy Reader.* New York: Routledge.

Freire, P. (1971) *Pedagogy of the Oppressed.* New York: Seabury.

McLaren, P. (1989) *Life in Schools: An Introduction to Critical Pedagogy and the Foundations of Education.* New York: Longman.Press.

What Is Anti-racist Education?

30

George J. Sefa Dei

Anti-racist education is a discursive and political practice addressing the myriad forms of racism and their intersections with other forms of oppression in schooling and education. It argues that in order to understand the true effects of race, we must acknowledge the way in which race intersects with other forms of difference: gender, class, sexuality, ability, language and religion. However, anti-racist education primarily addresses the systemic and institutional dimensions of racism and draws attention to less overt racist acts, lodged in individual actions, practices and beliefs. Anti-racist education makes an important distinction between race, ethnicity and culture. It is noted that many have found the word 'race' or 'racial' to be problematic, choosing instead to speak about 'ethnicity' or 'cultural' differences. Anti-racist education criticizes this approach. Race and racial differences, however constructed, matter in concrete ways. Naming them explicitly is very important for anti-racist education. It is crucial in anti-racist work to name race for what it is. Anti-racism education points out that race, like gender, class, ethnicity, religion, language and disability, is an important social category. It is a powerful marker of identity. As a society, we live our fears, hopes and anxieties in racial terms. Thus, we must confront race, racism and the ways in which power is evoked in school systems to disenfranchise particular groups. Rather than deny race and racial categories, anti-racist education challenges conventional interpretations of them.

While anti-racist education challenges all forms of racist acts, behaviours and practices in schools, critical anti-racist education focuses foremost on systemic racism and the racist politics of schooling. Within the school systems, structural racism revolves around certain ontological, epistemological and axiological foundations. For example, at the ontological level, our schools are seen as fair, value free and objective. At the epistemological level, it is argued that by working with 'merit,' 'excellence' and "thinking in hierarchies," educators and learners can arrive at the ontological foundation of fairness, objectivity and value free society. Axiologically, it is insisted that treating everybody equally (as in social justice for all) and discounting the qualitative value of justice (that is, its moral and ethical essence in contrast to its quantitative aspect), is the most appropriate thing to do. Equal opportunity and colour blindness are much heralded, despite the fact that these notions complicate racism by masking its real material and political effects and consequences. Critical anti-racist education challenges White power and its rationality for dominance. Critical anti-racist education resists racist and colonial privileges. The academic and political project of critical anti-racist education is to uncover how Western civilization scripts local communities through the fabrication of Whiteness and the policing of its corollary racial boundaries.

Anti-racist education also works with the notion of 'racialization' and 'racialized subjects' to identify social processes around race issues. Anti-racist education brings a complex meaning to race. While it is understood that race is not a static, bounded or fixed category and that the meaning of race evolves continually in different historical contexts, critical anti-racist practice also cautions us that the shifting meaning of race, and the experience of race as contextual, applies more to dominant groups than to those who are racialized as "non-Whites." Also, while anti-racism argues that race cannot be understood if decoupled from class, gender, sexuality, language and religion, critical anti-racist education, while drawing on these connections, highlights the saliency of race. That is, arguing that in a racialized society race trumps other forms of difference.

While all oppressions have certain things in common (e.g., they work within structures, are intended to establish material advantage and disadvantage, and also serve to create a self/other distinction), oppressions are not equal in their consequences. In other words, oppressions differ in their consequences and the burdens of oppression are not shared equally. The collective quest for solidarity in anti-oppression work can mask some underlying ambivalences and tensions when we fail to broach questions of power and privilege. In order to guard against these tensions, anti-racism does not seek to separate the politics of difference from the politics of race.

In our schools and classrooms today, many students have to contend with the everydayness of racism. This requires that educators pursue critical education vigorously to challenge power-laden encounters, which often times reveal an egregious display of White dominance and/or White supremacy. For the classroom practitioner, anti-racism insists each learner must be assisted to adopt a stance that advocates identifying, challenging and changing values, structures and behaviours that perpetuate systemic racism and other forms of oppression. In the context of schooling, the discourses of mosaic and multiculturalism, which may cherish difference and plurality, and promote an image of multiple, thriving, mutually respectful and appreciative ethnocultural communities, must be seen as inadequate. Anti-racism argues that while education, sharing and the exchange of knowledges are relevant, educators must implement mechanisms that redress injustice and seek fundamental structural and societal change. The problems of schooling are not simply manifest in intolerance and a lack of good will. The problems are questions of bias, discrimination, hatred, exclusion and violence. Rather than viewing racial prejudice as manifest simply in individual acts of bigotry and/or as violations of democratic rights, racism must be understood as an integral part of the social structure or social order.

Critical anti-racist education highlights the material and experiential realities of minoritized peoples in their dealings with the school system. Anti-racism also means learning about the experience of living with racialized identities, and understanding how students' lived experiences in and out of school, implicate youth engagement and disengagement from school. Anti-racism uncovers the ways in which race, ethnicity, class, gender, sexuality, ability, power and difference influence and are influenced by schooling processes. Anti-racism interrogates the processes of teaching, learning and educational administration as well as the ways in which they combine to produce schooling successes and failures for different bodies. Anti-racism opines that questions of power, equity and social difference are significant for learning outcomes and the provision of opportunities for all youth.

Further Readings

Dei, G. J. S. (1996) *Anti-Racism Education: Theory and Practice*. Halifax, NS: Fernwood Publishers.

Dei, G. J. S., James-Wilson, S. and Zine, J. (2002) Inclusive Schooling: *A Teachers' Companion to Removing the Margins*. Toronto, ON : Canadian Scholar's Press.

Lee, E. and Rey, M. O. (Eds.) (1997) *Beyond Heroes and Holidays: A Practical Guide to K-12 Anti-Racist, Multicultural Education and Staff Development*. Washington, DC.: Teaching for Change.

What Is Social Justice Education?

31 *Wendy Kohli*

The concept of social justice, like all concepts, cannot be elucidated adequately in the abstract. This is one of the contributions made to philosophical analysis by particular strands of feminist, critical and post-modern thought; they argue for *situating concepts in context*. A range of theorists maintain that engaging in critical reflection on social, political or ethical concepts, in the abstract, yields – more often than not – empty rhetoric rather than substantive, meaningful claims. These abstract concepts appear as disembodied "views from nowhere" with embedded assumptions of homogeneity and universality that serve to mask unequal social, economic and political relations.

If understanding occurs in particular contexts, then it follows that the meaning of these concepts is situated, *historicized*. Any *a priori* assumptions of fundamental commonality across different contexts need challenging. *Difference* has come to the table within political and social philosophy, with its resulting disruption and contestation. This does not mean, however, a situation of paralyzing incommensurability across different situations, but rather a need for negotiation of the *plurality* of meanings that exists. Traditional political and social philosophy, as well as the contributions by feminist/critical/postmodern theorists, can help illuminate the complexity of social justice for educators so that they may offer more compelling arguments for justice, freedom and equality in their respective contexts.

The dominant educational discourse of our time is characterized by technocratic, authoritarian, hierarchical, and even patriarchal language and politics. The conservative rhetoric of accountability and individual achievement has not thwarted the strength of the counter-discourse of progressive educational researchers, activists and teacher educators who are "educating for social justice." In fact, in the past two decades, despite the ascendancy of the New Right, social justice has gained widespread acceptance as a legitimate educational aim at different levels of the educational system, including in the elementary and secondary curriculum. Entire teacher education programs are informed by conceptual frameworks that embrace social justice as their defining purpose.

But this all begs the question. What do 'social justice' and "educating for social justice" mean? To what degree are we talking about the same thing from context to context, from purpose to purpose? Can we construct some common principles or definitions that will help clarify what we mean? If not, what are we to do when advocating for some of the worthy goals of social justice – such as equal educational opportunity, inclusive, multicultural schools, or ending homophobia?

Critical analysis is required to uncover the assumptions that inform our definition of social justice. Unpacking what we mean by *justice* and a *just society* is an obvious starting place. Different ideological positions lead to different conceptions of not only what justice is, but more fundamentally what a society is and who counts as a member of a society. Here we need only to be reminded of the traditional political categories of liberals, conservatives, and radicals (Marxists, for example) to see the contesting views on the relationship between the individual and society, the role of the government (state), and what individuals are entitled to as members of a given society. To what degree do we understand justice as a *political category* related to rights and responsibilities, and to what degree is it an *economic category* related to equitable distribution of/access to goods and opportunities? Where do *cultural* categories fit in to the situation? These varying positions affect our understandings of what it means to *promote* justice and what remedies will obtain for past or present injustices.

The concept of social justice took hold in liberal western democracies at the end of the nineteenth century when there was the opportunity and the obligation, both politically and economically, to press for more equality and freedom – and to address the tensions/contradictions of an emerging capitalist economy. This historically situated concept has come to assume a 'natural,' *universal* quality, when in fact it represents a *particular* liberal-capitalist worldview. The same can be said for the political philosophy that has informed much of the discourse on justice. Social contract theory, and its modern version, Rawlsian "distributive justice," takes for granted this liberal-capitalist worldview. Many Socialists and Marxists took issue with this liberal distributive paradigm because it did not provide a serious critique of capitalism. For these critics, *production,* including the processes and structures that controlled production, was the main focus of analysis, not distribution. They believed that it was not possible to have 'real' social justice if the economic system that shaped social and political life was fundamentally unjust.

Feminists have also provided powerful critiques of this dominant paradigm. For some feminists, the abstract, universal quality of social contract theory obscured the taken-for-granted institutionalized sexism that informed and supported a patriarchal view of justice. Still others argued that, as important as the fair distribution of goods and opportunities is, social justice should not be equated with distributive justice: social justice goes beyond that and addresses fundamental issues of oppression and domination. By introducing the concepts of oppression and domination, feminist political philosophers paid attention to the "social group," the identification one has to particular cultural groups, and the relative *privilege of groups* in a society. Scholars of color also offered a trenchant analysis of the racial underpinnings of our modern, liberal democracies and the fundamental inequalities and injustices that existed from the start.

Broadening the concept of social justice to include multi-cultural meanings, identities and differential power/privilege, affects our understandings of politics and political change. It also affects how we need to educate others about justice and injustice. Social justice education is a '*praxis*' that includes a theoretical account of oppression and privilege, as well as practical strategies for changing social institutions. Schools are primary sites for this critical transformation since they reproduce inequality. Educating students to overcome internalized forms of oppression – such as racism, sexism, classism and homophobia, offering them a framework for understanding the external structures that are the source of these different oppressions, and empowering students to become agents of change, are all important goals of social justice education.

Further Readings_____

Bell, L. (1997) Theoretical Foundations for Social Justice Education, in M. Adams, L.
    Bell & P. Griffin (Eds.), *Teaching for Diversity and Social Justice: A Sourcebook.*
    New York: Routledge.
Miller, D. (1999) *Principles of Social Justice.* Cambridge, MA: Harvard University Press.
Young, I. M. (1990) *Justice and the Politics of Difference*, Princeton, NJ.: Princeton
    University Press.

What Is Feminist Pedagogy?

32 *Frances A. Maher*

The term 'pedagogy' commonly refers to teaching practices: the approaches teachers use to convey their subject matter to students. "Feminist pedagogies" aim to foster equal access, participation, and engagement for all students in the learning process. Their practitioners seek to oppose sexism, racism, social class prejudice and homophobia as classroom barriers to equality. Moreover they wish to enable students, particularly female students, to be educated for personal awakening and growth as well as to pursue social equality and justice. While originally primarily conceived in terms of women's perspectives, feminist pedagogies increasingly reflect students' and teachers' multiple identities and positions in settings of educational diversity – identities given by class, race, culture, and age and other dimensions as well as gender.

The principles behind the development of feminist pedagogies in the last twenty years reflect many strands of progressive educational thought. These include the work of John Dewey and more recently the work of Paulo Freire in critical literacy. Feminist teachers, while sharing Dewey's and Freire's engagement with student empowerment, also diverge from these schools in that they claim a particular commitment to women students, a concern with gender as a category of analysis for their teaching practices, and the conviction that women and men (and by extension other diverse groups) might have different, even oppositional, educational needs and interests.

Feminist pedagogies also derive from the thirty-year long impact of feminist scholarship on the academy. As the academic disciplines have taken on the experiences of women, people of color, and other marginalized groups, so the classroom has become increasingly an arena for the intersection of these new and previously silenced perspectives. Like the field Women's Studies itself, feminist pedagogies are also rooted in the legacies of the 1960's women's liberation movements which engendered the consciousness-raising groups by which women began to explore and articulate their own experiences and feelings publicly for the first time. These groups bequeathed to formal educational settings, and to feminist pedagogy, an attentiveness to student personal experience, a respect for the emotions as a valid source of learning, and a view of the teacher as a facilitator and equal participant rather than a distant authority.

Finally feminist pedagogy emerged from the ongoing research on female students at all levels which showed that girls and women have been disadvantaged by the practices of male-dominated and hierarchically organized classrooms. Feminist theorists in the fields of education and psychology specifically suggested that traditional teaching approaches favor males; girls and women would benefit from classroom atmospheres which are collaborative rather than competitive, and concerned with 'connected' and relational, rather than separate, analytical and rational approaches to learning.

In weaving together these complex legacies and lessons, feminist teachers by the mid-1980s had evolved a variety of specific teaching methods. These included collaborative learning groups and projects, evoking student personal reactions and experiences through journals, shared classroom decision-making, student-led discussions, and many more.

However, in the past two decades, major upheavals in the feminist classroom have transformed the early models of feminist teaching. Women of color, working class women and lesbians pointed out that heterosexual white middle class academic feminists created women's studies scholarship in their own image, ignoring more marginalized and oppressed women just as male theory had ignored all women. The emphasis on sharing individual "personal experiences" tended to silence the women, often women of color, who would be the minority in any particular classroom. A classroom search for *commonalities* in the experiences of all women thwarted the evolution of theory from contradictory and different perspectives, leaving its construction to the dominant group - white heterosexual women - and leaving others at the margins.

In response, to these challenges, the more recent work in feminist pedagogy has embraced what may be called "pedagogies of difference," or "positional pedagogies." Differences of power, learning styles, cultural and class backgrounds and other variables that students and teachers bring to the classroom are the persistent stumbling blocks, once avoided by feminist teachers, where feminist pedagogies now begin. The goal is not to replicate these power relationships but to challenge and change them. For example, much work has recently been done on the concept of 'whiteness' and other positions of privilege; pedagogies of positionality encourage the excavations of privilege in the classroom. If white students come to see that whiteness is a position, just as is gender, then race and gender can be seen as relational and interactive: each side constructs the other in a constantly shifting dynamic which feminist teachers can work both to reveal and transform.

The acknowledgement of these dynamics of difference, whether of gender, race, culture, or pedagogical authority, illustrates the ongoing challenges faced by feminist teachers and the difficulties they encounter. Experimentation with collaborative classroom dynamics, positioning students as authorities, pushing them to articulate their varying positions in relation to a vibrant and growing literature continues, and feminist teachers are always "in process". Furthermore the current tensions in feminist theory persist – between the postmodern construction of 'woman' as a shifting product of relational discourses and an emphasis on the real oppression of many women. In the classroom, to see everyone as positioned is not to see every position as equally valid, but rather to uncover the complex and shifting relations of privilege that are masked by any one ideological position, especially that of "all women."

While classrooms reflect the power dynamics of the larger society, they also offer arenas to observe and challenge them. The increasing diversity of our populations makes for far richer and more complex classroom environments. It is in this fertile soil that we hope feminist pedagogies will continue to both struggle and flourish, and that the term "feminist pedagogy" will still retain its emancipatory possibilities.

Further Readings_____

Maher, F. A. & Tetreault, M. K. (2001) *The Feminist Classroom: Dynamics of Gender, Race and Privilege*. Expanded Edition. Lanham, MD: Rowman & Littlefield.

Ropers-Huilman, B. (1998) *Feminist Teaching in Theory and Practice: Situating Power and Knowledge in Poststructural Classrooms*. New York: Teachers College Press.

Weiler, K. (Ed.) (2001) *Feminist Engagements: Reading, Resisting and Revisioning Male Theorists in Education and Cultural Studies*. New York: Routledge.

What Is Citizenship Education?

33 *Eamonn Callan*

The ancient philosopher Aristotle defined the citizens of a state as those who are entitled to hold public office and exercise political power. Aristotle's definition is still sound even when it is applied to the conditions of large, technologically advanced liberal democracies. Although the prospects of any individual citizen occupying public office in a contemporary democracy may be slight, the right to seek office is still widely prized as basic to our status as citizens. More important still is the fact that as citizens in a democracy we control the political system through plebiscites and the election of officials.

The exercise of control over the state is not merely a right that citizenship entails; it is also a responsibility that may be discharged well or badly. To the extent that good political judgment is the outcome of what we are taught by others and teach ourselves it is an outcome of education. Therefore, it should not be surprising that the proper character of citizenship education has been a matter of philosophical discussion for as long as the nature of good government has been. The philosophical questions we can ask about citizenship education can be conveniently divided into disputes about its proper ends and the appropriate means to achieving those ends.

The ends of citizenship education are almost inevitably in dispute in contemporary democracies. The members of any such society subscribe to different religious and ethical ideals. We assume that toleration and mutual respect is the appropriate political response to this diversity. Therefore, we worry about the risk that state power will be used in the name of citizenship education to impose the beliefs and values of the majority, or even a powerful minority, on others. On the other hand, toleration and respect in the midst of diversity cannot be indiscriminate, and a reasonable worry is that without a common education that vigorously supports the institutions and values of free government, these will be vulnerable to steady decline. Citizenship education must chart a course between the accommodation of diversity and the mobilization of broad and deep support for basic political norms. Our disagreements arise not just because these two ends pull in different directions but because we interpret them differently.

One interesting issue in this regard is how we should interpret the norm of mutual toleration and respect. According to one familiar view, we can reliably respect the rights of others even when we are more or less thoroughly ignorant of their creed or culture, and we can tolerate ways of life that we fail entirely to understand. On that view, citizenship education requires very little in the way of knowledge about the sources of social diversity if respect and toleration are to be perpetuated from one generation to another. Alternatively, we may doubt that respect and toleration is really feasible when making complex choices as citizens in multicultural and religiously diverse societies if mutual ignorance and misunderstanding abound. In that event, we will claim that a substantial understanding of diversity is a necessary end for any citizenship education that is equal to the task of securing toleration and respect.

Another prominent source of controversy is the status of patriotism as an aim of citizenship education. Mass schooling has historically been closely connected with the project of "nation building," whereby states use education to build a strong sense of common identity among citizens rooted in patriotic sentiment. We typically regard patriotism as an important civic virtue when emotional attachment to our own nation or multination state is at issue. Nevertheless, the harm that misplaced patriotic sentiment can do is very obvious when we look at the misconduct of states *other* than our own. Once we recognize that, we cannot consistently deny that our own patriotism is invulnerable to a comparable corruption. The ever increasing interdependence between states that globalization has caused and the growing recognition that questions of justice between states are often as morally urgent as questions of justice within states have also fueled skepticism about patriotism as an end of civic education. Still, citizenship at the level of the state remains the primary venue for the exercise of political power, and that seems likely to remain so for the foreseeable future. The loss of patriotic attachment to the state might spur civic disengagement at that level. If that is true, patriotism may properly remain an important end of citizenship education, even if it must be taught in a way that discourages the evils with which it has been commonly associated.

Controversies about the best means to achieve particular civic educational ends will be in large part a matter for empirical investigation. But here too philosophy plays its part. First, certain forms of pedagogy may be ruled out by moral argument even when they are effective ways of achieving some desirable civic ends, and philosophy may be necessary to clarify that argument. The moral argument against indoctrination is an obvious case in point. Second, some educational ends will directly imply something about the content of the process through which they are achieved, and philosophical analysis will help to disclose these.

An interesting example here is what philosophers call "personal autonomy." This signifies an ideal of independent thought and choice that contrasts with both unreflective conformity and weakness of will. A common view is that responsible citizenship requires autonomy because citizens who vote without thinking for themselves subvert the very point of democracy as a means of equalizing power through the electoral system. If that is true, then citizenship education requires an education for autonomy. But that would seem to entail an educational process in which opportunities to exercise students' developing capacities for autonomy are gradually made available. Schools as we know them – as well as the other institutions that impinge on students' lives – provide little such opportunity.

The ends and means of citizenship education are matters of ongoing philosophical controversy. But that does not mean reflection on them is futile; it only means that reflection is difficult and that enduring disagreement is to be expected. They are questions on which all educators must take a stand. Whether the stand one takes is informed and reflective is up to us.

Further Readings_____

Callan, E. (1997) *Creating Citizens: Political Education and Liberal Democracy*. Oxford: Clarendon Press.

Gutmann, A. (1999) *Democratic Education*, rev. ed. Princeton, N. J.: Princeton University Press.

McDonough, K., & Feinberg, W. (2003) *Citizenship and Education in Liberal-Democratic Societies*. Oxford, U.K.: Oxford University Press.

What Is Spiritual Education?

34 *Daniel Vokey*

"What is spiritual education?" This question was central to a course recently offered at the University of British Columbia titled *Spirituality and Education in a Pluralistic World*. In the process of investigating what spiritual education is and could be, the participants in the course – graduate students from a variety of programs inside and outside the Faculty of Education plus myself as instructor – generated a long list of further questions. On top of that list was "What do we mean by *spirituality?*" because we needed to develop some shared understanding of the term to address the topic of spiritual education. Accordingly, we undertook to clarify how spirituality can be understood in relation to (a) religion; (b) belief in God; (c) the search for personal fulfilment and meaning in life; (d) rationality; (e) creativity and the imagination; (f) intuition and moral perception; (g) emotions such as caring, compassion, and sympathetic joy; (h) ethical judgment and moral conduct, including action in service of such ideals as social justice and freedom from oppression; and (i) evil.

One very common way of understanding *spirituality* is as a path or journey of personal transformation. There was no consensus among the course participants on what the ultimate destination of the spiritual journey might be. At the same time, a general theme that emerged from our reading and conversations was that spirituality concerns development *from* an initial narcissistic preoccupation with short-term pleasures and pains *to* a more wise and compassionate way of life arising from a profound sense of *connection* – connection with other people one-on-one and in community, with the natural world and its diverse non-human inhabitants, and/or with purposes, potentials, and powers beyond ego's limited concerns.

Once spirituality is understood in terms of personal transformation, then the question arises of whether or not it can be taught. Perhaps spiritual development proceeds more by trial and error than by instruction? Most of the participants in the course were educators, and many were teachers in K-12 public schools. Not surprisingly, then, we generally assumed that, although some bold travellers might find their way by their own lights, they would be more likely to progress on the path with an experienced guide, working with the maps and directions provided by one or more genuine spiritual traditions. We considered how spiritual teachers might assist the personal transformation of their students by introducing them to disciplines and practices that work with different dimensions of human experience, including sensations, perceptions, feelings, emotions, ideas, and direct intuitive insights.

Discussing such possibilities quickly resulted in more questions for our list – questions about how (if at all) we might individually or collectively distinguish between what helps and what hinders spiritual development. How (if at all) can we identify genuine spiritual teachers? How (if at all) can we identify which spiritual commitments and practices are truly beneficial and which are not? The difficulty we faced as a class was not that we found no answers to questions about which forms of education are and are not spiritually wholesome. Rather, the challenge was that we encountered many thoughtful answers that did not always agree. To whom should we pay heed?

Our discussions revealed that, in a pluralist liberal democracy such as Canada, advocates of spiritual and moral education both face a similar challenge. When it comes down to choosing particular beliefs and practices to promote, what different people will find conducive to spiritual or moral development will vary according to the different religious, philosophical, scientific, political, and cultural traditions that inform their points of view. Clearly, different traditions can offer one or more forms of spiritual education to those participating in the corresponding communities that embrace a particular understanding of the spiritual journey, its destination, and the allies and obstacles one is likely to encounter along the way. However, more questions need to be addressed to determine how (if at all) spirituality might legitimately inform teaching and learning in public, secular educational institutions. What are the respective rights of scholars, community leaders, teachers, students, and parents in deciding what is best for the spiritual or moral education of children? What are reasonable boundaries on the responsibilities of teachers and schools to promote such development? Do the potential benefits to students and their learning of attention to spirituality in schools outweigh the potential harms?

Notwithstanding the differences that exist among traditions and communities, both secular and religious, we did identify one way in which spirituality might legitimately inform teaching and learning in multicultural public schools, and that was through its potential contributions to the personal development of teachers. In particular, we discussed how at least some spiritual teachings and practices can help us enhance our ability to respect, appreciate, and learn from what is *Other*. This includes ideas and people that we might initially experience as unfamiliar, strange, and perhaps even somewhat intimidating or disagreeable. In my view, the ability to be open in this way is important because good teaching and learning depend so much upon positive relationships between teachers and students; and *modelling* virtuous attitudes, beliefs, and actions is the core of spiritual and moral education.

As you will have guessed, our discussion of the "inner landscape" of teachers added more questions to our long list. Can students perceive the degree of personal development of their teachers? Are there courses available for teachers that would promote such development? If not, should there be? If so, what form might they take? Do universities and colleges have an obligation to support the spiritual development of teachers-to-be? If so, why? We found that, although the conversations sparked by all these questions did not always produce definitive answers or universal agreement, they greatly enriched our understanding of what spiritual education could be, and of the conditions under which it was likely to be of benefit to students, teachers, and their communities. If our experience is any indication, such questions are worthy of serious consideration by educators inside and outside public schools.

Further Readings_____

Glazer, S. (Ed.) (1999) *The Heart of Learning: Spirituality in Education*. New York: Jeremy P. Tarcher.

Kessler, R. (2000) *The Soul of Education: Helping Students Find Connection, Compassion, and Character at School*. Alexandria, VA: Association for Supervision and Curriculum Development.

Palmer, P. (1998) *The Courage to Teach: Exploring the Inner Landscape of a Teacher's Life*. San Francisco: Jossey-Bass.

What Is Character Education?

35 *Michael Davis*

For the purposes of this chapter, *character* is the relatively settled general disposition of a person to do what is morally good. Rough synonyms for 'character' so understood are "good character," "moral character," "moral integrity," and 'virtue.'

Character can be analyzed into a set of *traits* – that is, so many narrower dispositions or virtues – courage, caring, honesty, responsibility, and so on. But character is not simply the sum of such traits. The traits must be organized in a certain way. There is a "unity of the virtues." So, for example, while everyone would count courage as a trait of good character, courage in an evil person does not seem to be a good trait. An evil person with courage is morally worse than he would be without it. He may dare what a coward would not.

Character *education* is any attempt a *school* makes to improve a student's character, that is, to make more likely than otherwise that the student will do what she should – not simply today but for many years to come. The long term – "many years" – is implicit in any claim to be educating *character*. By definition, short-term effects are not part of character. Character is a *settled* disposition. When someone we thought to have good character goes bad, we are more likely to cite some pre-existing 'flaw' (even if we never noticed it) than to admit that her character (once flawless) had been 'corrupted'. Once formed, character endures. In this respect, character seems to differ from both virtue and integrity; we are much more willing to admit that they can suffer decay or corruption.

Character education is a form of moral education. It differs from other forms of moral education in claiming to change character rather than simply to teach knowledge, skill, or judgment concerning matters moral (morality consisting of those standards we all – at our rational best – want everyone else to follow even if that would mean having to do the same). In practice, character education seems to take one of three forms (when it does not come as a mixture of them). These forms have no standard names, but we may call them: 1) moral development; 2) just-community education; and 3) character-trait education.

Moral development resembles education generally. Its focus is the classroom. It works by increasing student sensitivity to issues (by, say, pointing out instances where we must choose between discomfort and deception), by adding to what students know (such as ways to avoid deception without causing others discomfort), and by giving students a chance to apply what they know to 'problems' (what should you do if that happened to you?). The preferred method of moral development is guided discussion of problems requiring students to identify issues, develop options, make reasoned choice among the options, and defend the choices so made. Moral development tends to focus on method (thinking problems through), not on any pre-set conclusion ("stealing is bad"). Insofar as moral development improves the character of students, it does so by enhancing their intellectual resources, especially their knowledge of moral issues, skill at developing options, and ability to choose on the basis of publicly defensible reasons. The only character *trait* it is likely to instill is moral judgment, a kind of judiciousness. Lawrence Kohlberg is the seminal thinker in this tradition.

Just-community education attempts to shape student character through a civic apprenticeship. The school is turned into a "just community" in which (apart from matters of pedagogy) students and teachers democratically make policy and carry it out. Students are supposed to develop democratic virtues – tolerance, rationality, responsibility, concern for the common good, and so on – by practising them with the help of their teachers. The virtues are to be learned as a practical whole, not trait by trait. The classroom is only one locale in which just-community education goes on, perhaps not even the most important. John Dewey is the seminal thinker in this tradition.

Character-trait education treats character education as more or less analogous to physical education. Aristotle is said to have summarized the essential truth behind it: "We become just by the practice of just actions, self-controlled by exercising self-control, and courageous by performing courageous acts." Character-trait education shares with just-community education a concern to teach outside the classroom as well as within. It differs from just-community education (and moral development) in its concern to teach character by teaching specific traits. The chief sign that a school is engaged in character-trait education is a short list of specific 'traits', 'virtues', or 'values' to be taught.

Instituting a program of character education always risks controversy. For example, moral development is often attacked as "mere relativistic value clarification;" character-trait education, as "mere indoctrination." The best defense against such criticism is a well-conceived program. To prepare such a program, educators should consider the following three questions (among many others):

1. **Is the end in view morally appropriate?** It is, for example, not morally appropriate to develop 'patriotism' in students if that character trait is understood as doing whatever one's country asks. Blind obedience is not a virtue.

2. **Are the means morally appropriate?** One should not, for example, deliberately risk a student's life to teach character. Education cannot make morally permissible what is otherwise morally wrong.

3. **Is there evidence that the program will work?** To claim to teach character is to claim a long-term effect for one's teaching. The empirical evidence that moral development has a long-term effect on judgment is substantial. There is reason to believe that just-community education does much the same insofar as its practical discussions resemble the academic discussions of moral development. There is no evidence that

character-trait education teaches character traits (because there have been no long-term studies of its effects). Some methods of character-trait education can be justified for reasons having nothing to do with character, for example, less student misbehavior in school. But if the justification of a method is such short-term effects, it should not be described as character education. Character education should respect the truth.

Further Readings

Bebeau, M. J. et al. (1999) Beyond the Promise: A Perspective on Research in Moral Education, *Educational Researcher* 28 (4): 18-26.

Benninga, J. S., Berkowitz, M. W., Kuehn, P., & Smith, K. (2003). The Relation of Character Education and Academic Achievement in California Elementary Schools, *Journal of Research in Character Education*, 1 (1): 17-30.

Davis, M. (2003) What's Wrong with Character Education? *American Journal of Education*. 110 (1): 32-57.

What Is Vocational Education?

Paul Hager

A simple, but idealistic, answer might be that it is education that produces a committed and proficient workforce. The term 'committed workforce' captures the idea that vocational education should equip workers for a fulfilling work life. This implies that workers of all kinds should gain personal growth and satisfaction from their participation in work and in their community. This idea links to the traditional notion of a vocation as a calling. It suggests that work needs to be rewarding in more senses than mere monetary ones. This dimension of vocational education accords with the richness implied by the term 'education' as against 'training.' A 'proficient workforce' is the other key notion in the above characterisation of vocational education. This captures the idea that work performance should be at a consistently high level. Clearly, any satisfactory system of vocational education should meet the skill needs of the economy.

These idealistic considerations suggest that vocational education should be a central core of formal education systems. However, a visitor from another galaxy who had imbibed these ideas would be shocked to discover the reality of vocational education in Western education systems. Unfortunately, in the history of formal education, and especially since the industrial revolution, the role of vocational education has been very problematic. For various reasons, in the edifice of formal education, vocational education has occupied a less central position than the above idealistic account would suggest.

One reason is that the term 'vocational education' has been reserved to designate the vocational preparation of only those sectors of the labour market with perceived lower status. Thus higher education has been increasingly the arena for entry to professional and high status technical occupations, with vocational education as the alternative for those unable to gain entry to higher education. Thereby, the notion of vocational education has been steadily debased in comparison to the more desirable higher education. Hence much vocational education is often dismissed as mere training rather than as genuine education. As more high-level technical and administrative occupations have joined the ambit of higher education, a paradox has been created. If occupational earning power is taken to indicate vocational attractiveness of courses, then higher eduction is more vocational than is vocational education since its graduates earn more in the labour market.

It is true that recent policy interest in promoting educational pathways has started to create more links between higher education and vocational education. However, the traditional institutional segregation is underpinned and reinforced by various conceptual dualisms that have dominated much educational thought. Despite strong criticism of these dualisms by writers such as Dewey, their impact on educational thought and policy has remained remarkably durable. Two especially prominent conceptual dualisms that have shaped vocational education are:

1. MIND/BODY

Educational thought has been strongly shaped by the assumption that the prime function of education is the development of minds. This is a prominent legacy of Plato and Aristotle, for whom theoretical knowledge is superior to both practical and productive knowledge. It has remained prominent in later educational thought influenced by Cartesian ideas. If humans are essentially minds that incidentally inhabit bodies, then development of mind remains the prime educational focus. Likewise, if thinking is the essential characteristic of minds, it can be kept apart from non-essential characteristics like habits, emotion and conation. Hence the common assumption that the best type of learning concerns minds not bodies. So propositional (mind) learning is held to be more educational than skill (body) learning. The former is seen as education, the latter training. When pressed, few people really believe that, say, their automobile should be looked after by people who employ only physical skills with no thinking involved, yet much education policy and practice reflects the ongoing influence of the mind/body dualism. Recent narrow and restrictive approaches to developing competency standards for skilled occupations provide powerful testimony to this.

The implausibility of mind/body dualism has become increasingly clear as neuroscience has developed. Contra dualism, parts of human beings, such as minds or brains, are not the kinds of thing that can learn, reason, make decisions, etc. Rather, human beings, persons, do these things. Even though it is true that reasoning, for example, is a *function* of a person's mind or brain, it does not follow that the person's reasoning activities are explicable in terms of the brain alone, as Bennett and Hacker have recently shown.

2. THEORY/PRACTICE

The theory/practice dualism is an offshoot of the idea that the best learning resides in minds. Seeking to understand high level practice that appears to involve at least a modicum of cognitive content, e.g. the practice of various professionals, the theory/practice approach preserves the sovereignty of theory over practice by conceptualising practice as application of theory. This view, which seeks to reduce practice to theory, is sometimes called 'technical rationality.' As Gilbert Ryle pointed out in *The Concept of Mind*, it is false. However, theory/practice accounts of performance retain some support still, though they are increasingly viewed as implausible. Strong doubts come from research on expertise and the rise of the knowledge society, both of which emphasise the inescapability of valuable knowledge being created during work performance. Not all valuable knowledge is in the form of propositions that can be learnt in advance of practice. Some such knowledge is tacit and dispositional. These considerations cast doubt on the widely adopted front-end model of vocational preparation, which assumes that suitable formal education, completed in circumstances remote from the workplace, will provide the theoretical understanding sufficient for a lifetime of practice. Not surprisingly, the current era has been marked by increasing breakdown of the front-end model.

What might a richer notion of vocational education look like? It would be *holistic* in viewing vocational knowledge as including not just propositional understanding, but cognitive, conative and affective capacities as well as other abilities and learned capacities, such as bodily know-how and skills of all kinds. All of these are components conceivably involved in work performance which at its richest moments involves making and acting upon judgments. Such judgments holistically involve all of the above components and reflect a capacity for successful action in and on the world. The learning required for such judgments is an ongoing process, rather than an acquisition event completed at the start of a career.

Further Readings_____

Beckett, D. & Hager, P. (2002) *Life, Work and Learning: Practice in Postmodernity*. London: Routledge.

Bennett, M. R. & Hacker, P. M. S. (2003) *Philosophical Foundations of Neuroscience*. Malden. MA: Blackwell Publishing.

Winch, C. (1998) *The Philosophy of Human Learning*. London: Routledge.

What Is Accountability?

Ann B. Vibert

Quite recently a local newspaper reporter called to interview me for a story about the accountability – or, more accurately, about what he assumed was the *lack* of accountability – of the public education system and many employed in it. I asked what he meant by 'accountability', a question that gave him considerable pause, and as a consequence, the interview began and continued badly, the two of us pursuing the issue very much at cross purposes. It wasn't necessarily that we disagreed; we didn't get as far as disagreement. The problem lay much more in a *disconnection*, as though we were speaking different languages: I was trying to get at his sense of the term accountability (and also trying to unsettle it a bit), and he was trying to get a straight answer (just the facts, ma'am) in everyday language. Both of us believed that we were speaking in plain and ordinary language, and that the other, however unwittingly, was not.

This is a scenario very familiar to many of us in education these days – I have a colleague who says he just doesn't talk to his neighbours about the subject any more. It seems to me that there's a growing disconnect between *public* and *official* discourses in education and *academic* and *professional* discourses in education, to the extent that those of us inhabiting the latter are increasingly disinclined to talk to our neighbours. This is, of course, a dangerous and disconcerting phenomenon, if we take seriously the 'public' in public education. And at the heart of the disconnect, I think, lies this language of accountability and the clouds of meaning and intent it brings trailing along with it. Despite the reporter's objections, I think it is far from a waste of time to examine the question "what is accountability and why are we talking about it?"

Words, like people, reveal much about themselves by the company they keep; this is, in part, what is meant by the term 'discourse.' Words never come from nowhere to arrive in the public domain innocent of a history, a location, and a perspective and set of interests forged in both. The origins of the term accountability are revealed in the root of the word: it is a term that comes from count and counting, and probably more recently from accounting, the set of financial management practices by which the fiscal integrity of private businesses and corporations are audited. Like so much of the public discourse in education today, the term accountability, then, comes to us out of the field of business and management studies.

To avoid being dismissed as a knee-jerk business basher, let me say at the outset that business and management studies certainly have their place in the world. But, to borrow a concept from the rhetoricians, the language of business has achieved the status of a "god terminology." In rhetoric, "god terms" and "devil terms" refer to words that operate within particular discourses to silence debate by appeal to unquestionable goods or evils: pay attention, for instance, to the variable effects of the terms 'entrepreneurial' and 'socialist' in American public discourse currently. A discourse such as accountability, I am suggesting, carrying the automatic sanction of a god terminology, begs interrogation on that basis alone. Further, the notion that practices, processes, and perspectives formulated in and for private enterprise automatically benefit a public enterprise like education, with its very different purposes and objectives, is at least questionable.

So what is the company that the term accountability keeps? Words like "bottom line," "profit margin," 'efficiency,' 'productivity,' and "measurable outcomes" spring easily to mind. In business, accountability is, on the face of things, a straightforward matter: the enterprise is accountable to its share-holders for the bottom line, a measurable outcome clearly supported by productivity and certain efficiencies. Transferred to public education, the implication is that notions of accountability can cut through much hot air to arrive at a similar bottom line: education is accountable to its share-holders (the public) for the bottom line (educational quality). But in education, complexities immediately arise that don't necessarily pertain in the field of business. These complexities include questions like what do we mean by "quality education," how do we assess it, to what extent do we as a polity agree on what comprises a quality education and how it is assessed, and *which* public's (because there is more than one) interests are best represented in our answers to these questions? These complexities are, of course, the enduring central questions at the heart of the whole undertaking of public education; they are the very debates that inform the history, philosophy, sociology, and psychology of education; they are, in short, the study of education itself. The discourse of accountability, with its attendant efficiencies and measurable outcomes, sweeps aside these questions as minor irrelevancies, pretending a world in which we already all know, agree upon, and can straightforwardly measure the answers to these perplexing questions. It is in this manner that accountability appears not to be about education at all, but about something else altogether.

One might explore this "something else" by returning to the root of the word accountability, and its connections to accounting. Here, recent cases suggest that even in the business world, notions of accountability may not always live up to claims to integrity and quality assurance. It was, after all, the practice of accounting that made possible the huge swindle that was Enron, as well as several similar corporate frauds. In these cases, accountability was not about integrity and quality at all, but about precisely the opposite, about the misleading *appearance* of integrity and quality. We need not, then, be surprised by the consequences of accountability discourses for integrity and quality in schooling: teaching to the test, raising standardized test scores by inviting the poor kids to stay home, producing banal mission statements and binders full of meaningless statistics, and planning for improvement rather than improving, are all we should expect when it is the *appearance* of quality we're after. I believe it is not 'accountability' we want in education, but 'responsibility,' a morally and ethically nuanced term that preserves the dignity and complexity of the work.

In the end, I suggested to the reporter above that my own "bottom line" is that schools may be too accountable to some 'publics' (those with power and privilege) and not nearly accountable enough to others (marginalized communities). He found this observation interesting, and readily supplied examples in terms of which schools get closed and which schools stay open in his own city. Interesting as the point was to him, however, he closed the interview by observing that it was really beside the point on the topic of accountability in education. Such is the power of discourse.

Further Readings_____

Blackmore, J. (2002) Is It only 'What Works' that 'Counts' in New Knowledge
    Economies? Evidence-based Practice, Educational Research and Teacher
    Education in Australia, *Social Policy & Society* 1 (3): 257-66.

Corbett, M. (2004) Knowing a Duck from a Goose: The Real World of Education in
    an Age of Smoke and Mirrors, *Our Schools/Ourselves* 13 (2): 95-122.

Kohn, A, & Shannon, P. (Eds.) (2002) *Education, Inc.: Turning Learning into a Business.*
    Portsmouth, N.H.: Heinnemann.

What Is Urban Education?

R. Patrick Solomon

I deally, urban education provides a curriculum and pedagogy that increases
the life opportunities and the practice of responsible citizenship of those
residing in urban communities. Historically, such spaces have been labelled
as "inner city" and low-income and characterized as high density, high
diversity, migrancy and transience, limited job opportunities and high
unemployment, limited social services, assisted housing, pathological and
wealth depleting. Increasingly, such spaces proliferate in pockets of large
metropolitan areas and have acquired labels such as "the new suburban
ghettos" with similar characterization as that of traditional urban enclaves. As
world populations become more urbanized by the movement of rural
dwellers, immigrant and refugee groups seeking better life opportunities in
cities, urban educators must respond to the many challenges posed by the
schooling of these emergent groups. Urban education for equity, diversity
and social justice reconceptualizes such communities as culturally rich,
wealth generating and potentially transformative. From such a perspective,
urban educators must address such wide-ranging learning needs as: the use
of language and literacy skills new urban groups bring to school (for example,
the non-mainstream dialects and native languages of immigrant students);

the acquisition of new language and literacy skills needed to function in their new multilingual environments and the broader global world; and the development of cultural competencies urban dwellers require to function across social, cultural, economic and institutional boundaries. Such a curriculum moves beyond the celebration of cultural differences to critically explore the factors that give rise to, and sustain, such oppressive and debilitating acts as racism, ethnocentrism, classism, homophobia, sexism and ableism that are often more concentrated and visible in urban than non-urban spaces.

Central to urban education curriculum is the development and use of community knowledge as legitimate and authentic. Such generative knowledge represents the lives and experiences of those urbanites who construct it. Urban education frowns upon the imposition and centralization of exclusive knowledge forms generated elsewhere by curriculum designers. This brings into question imported, standardized curriculum that preoccupies the standards movement in school reform. The subsequent testing and certification of such knowledge has led to a massive disenfranchisement of urban youth. Clearly linked to an inclusive curriculum that integrates curriculum content generated in urban communities are pedagogical approaches that engage students in collectivist and interdependent learning: students, classmates and teacher facilitator engage each other in the pedagogical process. This kind of pedagogy distances itself from the popular competitive individualism that is encouraged and rewarded in schooling practices for the global economic marketplace. This new pedagogy of community moves away from the notions of externally imposed discipline and control that have traditionally restricted and penalized interactivity in urban classrooms.

A key objective of urban education is to develop the social and cultural capital of the community. Researchers such as Robert Putman argue that the interpersonal relationships developed in neighbourhoods have significant impact on their economic productivity, viability and prosperity, their health and safety and their overall quality of life. Urban educators must therefore be creative in helping inner city, economically poor residents develop the social networking skills such as reaching across "social difference," collaboration, negotiation, maintaining stability, forming a strong liaison with social, cultural and academic institutions needed for community growth.

To achieve this goal, urban education must transgress the traditional institutional borders of schools and link with community-based organizations; for example, churches, service clubs, social service agencies, and youth clubs, to form collaborative networks. Key to school-community linkages are teachers who must build a trusting and productive relationship with low-income and economically poor parents. Teachers as genuine capacity-builders in urban schools and communities can only be developed through preparation programs that utilize the community as a site of learning to teach. That is, moving beyond the traditional institutional sites of the university and the practicum school and engaging the community in experiential learning. Educational philosophers such as John Dewey and Paulo Freire advocate an active and constructive participation in the life of the community in order to develop its capacity. Valuable lessons learned about the needs, resources and aspirations of communities help educators develop a culturally relevant pedagogy. Students develop social relationships with their teachers outside of the school/classroom setting; teachers develop better insights into the lives and challenges of inner city community residents, and communities develop their social capital by virtue of teacher involvement. Because of the traditional "hidden curriculum" of schools to maintain and reproduce dominant, middle class values and ideologies in urban, inner city schools, this progressive school-community border crossing by educators and cultural workers is not only good urban education but good education.

Urban education is ceaselessly challenged about its limits and possibilities. Can progressive urban education reverse the high drop-out/push out rates of students, boost their academic achievements, increase school safety, develop the social capital of neighbourhoods and reduce the "savage inequalities" between the 'haves' and the 'have-nots'? Traditionally, urban, inner city schools have systematically reproduced minimally educated assembly line workers at the bottom of the socio-economic hierarchy. In an era of more technologically advanced systems of production that demands higher quality of education, urban schools simply produce a working class without work. The task of urban education, therefore, becomes one of preparing students to maximize their potential to acquire meaningful, productive occupations within and beyond their communities. Equally important is their development as responsible and participating citizens in a democratic society.

How may urban education for social justice reduce school bureaucracy that stifles innovation, creativity in the workplace and the professional growth of teachers? How may we reduce the high departure rate of teachers who have the potential to make a difference in urban schools but do not stay long enough to be effective change agents? It is well argued by critics that urban school reform strategies cannot be effective or sustainable without parallel macro-level reform of the socio-economic and political structures in which urban schools operate. If stakeholders inside and outside schools are invested in, and benefit from, the structural inequities of urban schools and communities, from where will the moral authority come to disassemble such structures? Urban educators must assume the roles of activists and cultural workers and link forces with those George Counts labelled as social reconstructionists; those who use schools to build a new social order rather than those who maintain urban schools simply to reflect the social order. To accomplish this, however, requires a teacher preparation that moves beyond subject instruction, beyond the images of urban schools as dangerous and foreboding places, to focus more so on the larger social, economic and political structures that maintain urban communities in marginal, inequitable existence. However, progressive experiments and pilot projects informed by Freire and other visionaries have demonstrated that the negative characterization of urban spaces can be dramatically reversed by those with the vision, political will and the moral servitude to intervene. Urban school transformation can be realized by communities with social capital working in collaboration with enlightened educators and policy makers at the school and district levels.

Further Readings

Anyon, J. (1997) *Ghetto Schooling: A Political Economy of Urban Educational Reform.* New York: Teachers College Press.

Murrell Jr., P. C. (2001) *The Community Teacher: A New Framework for Effective Urban Teaching.* New York: Teachers College Press.

Yeo, F. L. (1997) *Inner-city Schools, Multiculturalism, and Teacher Education: A Professional Journey.* New York: Garland Publishing.

What Is the Marketization
39 of Education?

Kenneth J. Saltman

The 'marketization' of education refers to the transformation of public schooling on the model of the market. This transformation can be understood as comprising at least two dimensions: economic and cultural.

In an economic sense, reforming public schooling on the model of the market has involved introducing business and for-profit endeavours into a realm that has historically been publicly owned and controlled. These for-profit initiatives include the steady rise of school commercialism such as sponsored educational materials, advertisements in textbooks, in-class television news programs that show mostly commercials, soft drink vending contracts, and other attempts to hold youth as a captive audience for advertisers. School commercialism is a small part of the marketization of education. Other initiatives include companies running public schools for profit. This is sometimes referred to as "performance contracting" and it involves companies contracting with schools or school districts. Major market-based initiatives include for-profit charter schools, market-based voucher schemes, and the rise of the EMO or Educational Management Organization. In addition to the aforementioned, these companies hold a number of for-profit educational enterprises, including test publishing, textbook publishing, tutoring services, curriculum consultancies, educational software development, publication, and sales, toy making, and other companies.

In the U.S. the ESEA law ("No Child Left Behind") has encouraged marketization by investing billions of public dollars in the charter school movement, which is fostering privatization with over three quarters of new charter schools being for-profit. It is also requiring high-stakes testing, 'accountability' and remediation measures that are shifting resources away from public school control and into control by test and textbook publishing corporations and remediation companies. Despite a number of failed experiments with performance contracting in the U.S. in the 1980's and 1990's, for-profit education companies and their advocates continued to claim that they could operate public schools better and cheaper than the public sector. On the face of it this claim appears counter-intuitive: how could an organization drain financial resources to profit investors and still maintain the same quality that the organization had with the resources that could be paying for more teachers, books, supplies, and upkeep? Evidence appears on the side of intuition. To date the evidence shows that it is not possible to run schools for profit while adequately providing resources for public education. This has been equally true whether the profit model is vouchers, charters, or performance contracting. Nonetheless, the business sector, right-wing think tanks in and outside of academia, and corporate media continue to call for market-based approaches to public schooling.

Advocates of for-profit companies running schools rely on a number of arguments for their economic claims: 1) the larger the company becomes the more it can benefit from "economies of scale" to save costs through, for example, volume purchasing; 2) the private sector is inherently more efficient than the public sector because for-profit companies must compete with other companies; and 3) the private sector is more efficient because the public sector is burdened by regulations and constraints such as teachers unions and the protections that they afford teachers that only get in the way of efficient delivery of educational services. Proponents often justify commercialism and other for-profit initiatives on the grounds that they provide much needed income for under funded public schools. However, even the business press by 2002 recognized that education is not good business: schools have too many variable costs for economies of scale to work; business would have to be spectacularly efficient to allow for quality and skimming of profits for executives while Enron, Worldcom, Martha Stewart, and The Edison Schools show just how inefficient business can be; far from regulations being a hindrance they provide necessary protections against abuse of teachers' labour while providing financial transparency. As the largest ever experiment in marketization, The Edison Schools overworked teachers, mis-reported earnings, mis-reported test scores, counselled out low-scoring students, cheated on tests to show high performance to potential investors, and as they approached bankruptcy time and again, they revealed just how precarious and unaccountable the market imperatives can be when applied to education.

The cultural aspect of marketizing education involves transforming education on the model of business, describing education through the language of business, and the emphasis on what has been termed the "ideology of corporate culture" that involves making meanings, values, and identifications compatible with a business vision for the future. The business model appears in schools in the push for standardization and routinization in the form of emphases on standardization of curriculum, standardized testing, methods-based instruction, teacher de-skilling, scripted lessons, and a number of approaches aiming for "efficient delivery" of instruction. The business model presumes that teaching, like factory production, can be ever speeded up and made more efficient through technical modifications to instruction and incentives for teachers and students, like cash bonuses. Holistic, critical, and socially-oriented approaches to learning that understand pedagogical questions in relation to power are eschewed as marketization instrumentalizes knowledge, disconnecting knowledge from the broader political, ethical, and cultural struggles informing interpretations and claims to truth, while denying differential material power to make meanings.

Concomitant with neoliberal ideology, business metaphors, logic, and language have come to dominate policy discourse. For example, advocates of privatizing public schools often claim that public schooling is a 'monopoly,' that public schools have 'failed,' that schools must 'compete' to be more 'efficient,' and that schools must be checked for 'accountability' while parents ought to be allowed a 'choice' of schools from multiple educational providers as if education were like any other consumable commodity. Shifting public school concerns onto market language frames out public concerns with equality, access, citizenship-formation, democratic educational practices, and questions of whose knowledge and values constitute the curriculum.

Marketization threatens to undermine the public mission and public dimensions of public schooling by redefining schooling in private ways. This has potentially dire implications for societies theoretically committed to public democratic ideals by undermining civic education and collective public action. Instead marketization fosters hyper-individualism, consumerism, and a social Darwinist ethic thereby expanding the worst dimensions of the market into the public space of school. Market language and justifications for schooling eradicate the political and ethical aspects of education. For example, within the view of marketization, students become principally consumers of education and clients of teachers rather than democratic citizens in the making who will need the knowledge and intellectual tools for meaningful participatory governance; teachers become deliverers of services rather than critical intellectuals; knowledge becomes discrete units of product that can be cashed in for jobs rather than thinking of knowledge in relation to broader social concerns and material and symbolic power struggles, the recognition of which would be necessary for the development of genuinely democratic forms of education.

Further Readings

Boyles, D. (Ed.) (2004) *Schools or Markets?: Commercialism, Privatization and School-Business Partnerships*. New York: Lawrence Earlbaum and Associates.

Molnar, A. (2005) *School Commercialism*. New York: Routledge.

Saltman, K. (2000) *Collateral Damage: Corporatizing Public Schools – a Threat to Democracy*. Lanham, M.D.: Rowman & Littlefield.

What Is Zero Tolerance?

Ronnie Casella

There is no single definition of zero tolerance. There is zero tolerance for domestic violence, zero tolerance for drugs, zero tolerance for drunk driving, zero tolerance for school violence, and so on. Even within the realm of zero tolerance for school violence, the concept has several meanings and is used in different ways. It can reflect a general feeling among teachers and administrators that they take a "no nonsense" stand on student misbehavior and crackdown on unruly students. Zero tolerance is also political rhetoric, used by politicians and administrators to convince a wary public that their schools are safe and that authorities are getting serious about violence.

However, since the passing of the Gun-Free Schools Act in 1994, in the United States, zero tolerance has been codified in federal law, and has therefore become a more concrete policy dealing with weapons, fights, drugs, misbehavior, and threats of violence in schools. Though the Gun-Free Schools Act does not include the phrase "zero tolerance," the original law mandated that students caught with a firearm in school be expelled for no less than 180 days, and therefore laid the groundwork for schools' implementation of zero tolerance policies.

Since the enactment of the Gun-Free Schools Act, amendments have been made to the law to extend the legislation's application. In 1995, the word 'firearms' was amended to read 'weapons.' This made it possible for school personnel to expel for the full 180 days students in possession of not only firearms, but also the broader category of 'weapons,' and even items that could be used as weapons, such as nail files, fireworks, and pocket knives. As decision-makers in states and municipalities adopted the policy, they too included less serious violations punishable by zero tolerance standards, including fighting, threats of violence, graffiti, and general misbehavior.

Zero tolerance in schools is congruent with other national crime policies based on what some criminologists call "preventative detention." Like habitual-offender statutes, minimum sentencing laws, and "sexual predator" statutes (which force inmates to serve longer prison terms if they are deemed still dangerous at the end of their sentences), zero tolerance policy attempts to prevent violence by punishing individuals based on their perceived potential for violence. It reflects a general trend in crime policy in the United States to prevent future violations through the incarceration and control of potentially dangerous offenders. As with other crime policies of the 1990s, zero tolerance policy supports harsh judicial discipline.

While the policy rationale for zero tolerance can be found in the Gun-Free Schools Act, the theoretical rationale for the policy is based on rational choice theory. In criminology, rational choice theory states that individuals choose among a number of options of behavior and that their final choice is a rational one that involves the weighing of benefits versus consequences. If consequences are harsh, people are less likely to commit crimes. On the other hand, if benefits outweigh the consequences, people will pursue the benefits. Zero tolerance aims to convince youths to make the "rational choice" not to act inappropriately; it increases consequences to convince the rational thinker that, in a sense, the crime is not worth the time.

The only major restriction to zero tolerance policy in schools in the United States is the Individuals with Disabilities Education Act (IDEA), which is the major federal legislation overseeing the rights of students with disabilities. To some extent, IDEA limits the application of zero tolerance policy, especially as it relates to suspension, expulsion, and out-placements, but only to a point. Before the 1997 reauthorization of IDEA, a student with a disability could be removed from school for up to 45 days to an interim alternative educational setting for carrying a firearm. While this placed a restriction on the Gun-Free Schools Act, which stated that students should be expelled for 180 days for the same violation, the 1999 regulations that were mandated two years after the reauthorization modified this provision. Under the revised law, students in special education programs who have been found with any weapon (not just a firearm), or possess, use, sell, or solicit drugs in school or at school functions, as well as disabled students determined by a hearing officer to be so dangerous that the student's behavior is "substantially likely to result in injury to the child or others" – these students can also be suspended for up to 45 days. Additionally, these out-placements can be extended in 45 day increments if it is determined by a hearing officer that the student still poses a risk.

Supporters of zero tolerance policy emphasize that many forms of violence prevention are needed in a school, and that zero tolerance is one of them – that zero tolerance was never meant to be the sole means of discipline in a school. Most support a combination of zero tolerance with other violence prevention and conflict resolution programs. Those in favor of the policy also view zero tolerance as a way of heading off potential violence, of being strict but also consistent, and as a logical response to shootings in schools in the 1990s, which was when most schools began implementing the policy. Critics claim that the policy targets poor people of color and causes the derailment of students as they are suspended and expelled in greater numbers and for less serious infractions. Research has shown that zero tolerance policy affects some groups more than others, especially those who are poor, in urban areas, and who are Latino, Native American, or African-American. For poor students and marginalized students of color, zero tolerance adds another risk factor to lives that are already overburdened with risk factors.

Further Readings_____

Ayers, W., Dohrn, B., & Ayers, R. (2001) *Zero Tolerance: Resisting the Drive for Punishment in our Schools.* New York: The New Press.

Casella, R. (2001) *At Zero Tolerance: Punishment, Prevention, and School Violence.* New York: Peter Lang.

Devine, J. (1996) *Maximum Security: The Culture of Violence in Inner-City Schools.* Chicago: University of Chicago Press.

Notes on Contributors

Brenda Almond is Emeritus Professor of Moral and Social Philosophy, University of Hull, UK.

Heesoon Bai is Associate Professor, Faculty of Education, Simon Fraser University, Burnaby, British Columbia, Canada.

Sharon Bailin is Professor, Faculty of Education, Simon Fraser University, Burnaby, British Columbia, Canada.

Megan Boler is Associate Professor of Education, Department of Theory and Policy Studies, Ontario Institute for Studies in Education, University of Toronto, Ontario, Canada.

David Bridges is Professorial Fellow at the University of East Anglia and Chair of the Von Hugel Institute and Fellow of St. Edmond's College, University of Cambridge, UK.

Nicholas C. Burbules is Grayce Wicall Gauthier Professor, Department of Educational Policy Studies, University of Illinois, Urbana-Champaign, USA.

Eamonn Callan is Professor of Education, Stanford University, California, USA.

David Carr is Professor of Philosophy of Education, Moray House School of Education, University of Edinburgh, Scotland.

Ronnie Casella is Associate Professor of Secondary Education and Educational Foundations, Central Connecticut State University, USA.

Antonia Darder is Professor of Educational Policy Studies and Latino/Latina Studies, University of Illinois, Urbana-Champaign, USA.

Michael Davis is Senior Fellow at the Center for the Study of Ethics in the Professions, and Professor of Philosophy, Illinois Institute of Technology, Chicago, USA.

George J. Sefa Dei is Professor and Chair, Department of Sociology and Equity Studies, Ontario Institute for Studies in Education, University of Toronto, Ontario, Canada.

Pradeep A. Dhillon is Associate Professor, Department of Educational Policy Studies at the University of Illinois, Urbana-Champaign, USA.

Maureen Ford is Assistant Professor, Department of Theory and Policy Studies, Ontario Institute for Studies in Education, University of Toronto, Ontario, Canada.

Ronald David Glass is Associate Professor of Education, University of California, Santa Cruz, USA.

Paul Hager is Professor of Education, University of Technology, Sydney, NSW, Australia.

Sophie Haroutunian-Gordon is Professor and Director, Master of Science in Education Program, School of Education and Social Policy, Northwestern University, Illinois, USA.

William Hare is Professor of Education, Mount St. Vincent University, Halifax, Nova Scotia, Canada.

Michael Jackson was for many years Professor of Education at Memorial University of Newfoundland and Bishop's University, Quebec, Canada, and is now retired.

Wendy Kohli is Associate Professor of Curriculum and Instruction, Fairfield University, Connecticut, USA.

Frances A. Maher is Professor of Education, Wheaton College, Norton, Massachusetts, USA.

Michael Matthews is Associate Professor, School of Education, University of New South Wales, Sydney, Australia.

The late **Terence McLaughlin** was Professor of Philosophy of Education, Institute of Education, University of London, UK.

Nel Noddings is Lee Jacks Professor of Education Emerita, Stanford University, California and Adjunct Professor of Philosophy and Education, Teachers College Columbia, New York, USA.

William F. Pinar is Professor and Canada Research Chair, Department of Curriculum Studies, University of British Columbia, Vancouver, British Columbia, Canada.

John P. Portelli is Professor of Education and Co-Director of the Centre for Leadership and Diversity, Department of Theory and Policy Studies, Ontario Institute for Studies in Education, University of Toronto, Ontario, Canada.

Emily Robertson is Associate Dean of Education and Dual Associate Professor of Education and Philosophy at Syracuse University, New York, USA.

Jim Ryan is Professor of Education and Co-Director of the Centre for Leadership and Diversity, Department of Theory and Policy Studies, Ontario Institute for Studies in Education, University of Toronto, Ontario, Canada.

Kenneth Saltman is Assistant Professor of Education, DePaul University, Chicago, Illinois, USA.

Carolyn Shields is Professor and Head of the Department of Educational Organization and Leadership, University of Illinois, Urbana-Champaign, USA.

Harvey Siegel is Professor and Chair of the Department of Philosophy at the University of Miami, Florida, USA.

Douglas J. Simpson is Professor and holder of the Helen DeVitt Jones Chair in Teacher Education, Texas Tech University, Lubbock, Texas, USA.

Richard Smith is Professor of Education and Director of the Combined Degrees at the University of Durham, UK.

R. Patrick Solomon is Associate Professor, Faculty of Education, York University, Toronto, Ontario, Canada.

Paul Standish is Professor of Educational Studies, University of Sheffield, UK.

Shirley R. Steinberg is the Program Head of Graduate Literacy, Brooklyn College, USA and also teaches at the CUNY Graduate Center in Urban Education.

Candace Jesse Stout is Professor of Art Education, Ohio State University, Columbus, Ohio, USA.

Charlene Tan is Assistant Professor at the National Institute of Education, Nanyang Technological University, Singapore.

Barbara Thayer-Bacon is Professor of Philosophy of Education, University of Tennessee, Knoxville, Tennessee, USA.

Ann B. Vibert is Associate Professor of Education, Acadia University, Wolfville, Nova Scotia, Canada.

Daniel Vokey is Assistant Professor, Department of Educational Studies, Faculty of Education, University of British Columbia, Vancouver, British Columbia, Canada.